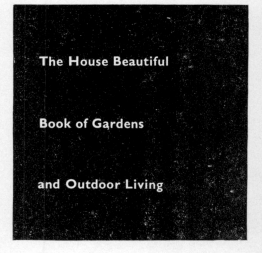

The House Beautiful

Book of Gardens

and Outdoor Living

The House Beautiful

Book of

Gardens

and Outdoor

Living

by Joseph E. Howland

Doubleday & Company Inc

BLACK & GOLD

Library of Congress Catalog Card Number 57–11740
Copyright © 1958 by The Hearst Corporation
All Rights Reserved
Designed by Clifford S. Smith
Printed in the United States of America
First Edition

1020835

Contents

5

Introduction

This book is essentially one of ideas, one that presents pictorially the results of the plans and hopes of men and women throughout the country. It shows in detail how imagination became almost the means themselves, in many instances, to overcome problems of site, contour, soil, climate, and the pocketbook. No particular part of the country is exhibited in preference to another; areas of topographical and climatic extremes have been given similar attention, for each presents its own requirements and problems, each encourages persons living on its soil to visualize, plan, and describe tangibly to himself his place on it.

At midpoint of the twentieth century Americans show, more than ever before, an intense, abiding interest in lessening the confinements of indoor living, going to immense effort and expense to bring to their daily lives those benefits of the outdoors that were once mainly within the reach of the well-to-do. A tremendous complex of social factors has, with startling speed, brought about a complete reversal, in many ways, of the individual's attitude and relation to his immediate social and geographic environment. Among the factors involved are the increase of income, with its accompanying raising of the standard of living, the great outward expansion from the city—suburban living—not quite able to keep up with itself in the rush away from the metropolis but still part of the city's pulse, an unparalleled urge for creating and buying what is beautiful or is widely believed to be beautiful, in possessing commodities that were obtainable, just a few years ago, only at high cost. Leisure, too, more so now than at any other period in the nation's history, has gained great stature and has caused the individual to surround himself with myriad requirements—necessities, luxuries—of indoor-outdoor living. America now sees itself as having effected social changes, not so greatly in a few separate extremes as in the over-all pattern, so that architecture and building, transportation and communication, all bear toward each other new, evolving relationships, created by, and affecting, the individual.

With the growing desire to be closer to the land and its benefits, Americans build houses that seem to rise from the ground itself, that blend in form and material, that frequently eliminate lines of wall and foundation that traditionally have divided the house from the land. It is easy to understand, then, the fact that the garden has achieved in this country its increasing importance. The trend has been, not to create strong contrasts between garden and house, but to harmonize, to complement the natural with the manmade. Today the garden may be considered in new lights—as integral living space, as a room open to the sky, as part of the house. Advances in design and in the techniques of construction have made this possible. Mass production, marketing, transportation in industrialized America have brought these advances to the doorstep of the homeowner, most particularly in the ever-broadening network of suburban living. The aggressive use of expanses of glass as stationary or sliding walls that can insulate, intensified use of the many new strong and durable construction materials have recently had widespread effect upon indoor-outdoor relationships. Hand in hand with the potentials of these new materials runs a new concept of light in its value to body and soul. Today winter's wall may easily become summer's invisible line between house and garden. The roof may appear to fade as the open construction of the terrace supplants it. Terrace and living room may achieve a oneness in a matter of seconds, disallowing the senses to note when, exactly, one has ended and the other begun. The house may flow into the outdoors to gain space, both visual and actual.

There are many aspects to be considered in the interplay of these new relationships of form, location, material:

Color, with its infinity of uses—in solid mass, in combination, in small but significant touches—seems now to enjoy a vogue so great as to suggest that what went before was an austerity. Color can be everywhere around the gardener, the homeowner—in clusters of flowers and in blooming shrubs, on walls, fences, and windbreaks, pavements and terraces, steps, on pillar and post—often appearing to defy the established bearing of ordered nature to men's constructions, but more often being the result of the individual's freedom and honest fancy with given materials.

Shadow and darkness now appear to be tools of design that are useful as well as pleasing to the eye, and that can often be as important as form and color, creating, among other things, intended patterns of the geometric and the whimsical.

Design in gardens, for so many years the realm of the owners of broad lands and of the great landscape architects, now seems to have upon it only the restrictions of a person's desires and of good taste, paying less heed to symmetry and formality, to the stance of the four-walled house against its earthy opposite. The heyday of America's English garden, the Italian and French gardens, once afforded only by the estate owner, is now past. Freedom of form, whether tangibilized by natural or man-made materials, is the prerogative of everyone to do with, right or wrong, what he will. Design of both house and garden tends more, now, to follow the contours of the site, and it has become almost a point of dedication for both the amateur gardener and the professional to make full use of existing trees and shrubs and of natural formations, rather than to make obvious nature's bending to man's projects. Garden design has changed more slowly, perhaps, than other aspects of the home because the tried and tested generally seem, to the new homeowner, to indicate the easiest ways to achieve some immediate results, and frequently little forethought is given to innovations in garden planning that are in keeping with advances in architecture and construction. The successful unconventional garden is generally the handiwork of people who themselves may once have adhered unquestioningly and closely to long-established modes of gardening.

The heart of the garden—trees, shrubs, flowering plants—may now be abundantly full in nearly all parts of the country in a variety of shape, size, and color previously undreamed of. Research has resulted in added strength and durability in the fruits of the earth; new techniques and products, growth inducers and fertilizers, ensure lusty growth and often a profusion of color greater, it might seem, than nature intended. It is now possible to grow plants in environments that were once not hospitable. Importations from the rest of the world are now available for adaptation. There is now an emphasis on the planting of evergreens, for their capacity to show luxuriance at all seasons often weighs more heavily in their favor than do "flower shows," which, though satisfying or spectacular, are at best of comparatively short duration.

Much progress has been made recently by the homeowner in the planning of his garden. Books and magazines have aided him considerably in avoiding certain pitfalls to which inexperience, almost inevitably, led him. To a large extent, however, the homeowner with an idea can ensure his planning, eliminate costly results of trial and error, by enlisting the services of experienced professional garden designers. The past several years have seen the emergence of skilled, knowledgeable craftsmen whose interest in small gardens refutes the belief that professional landscaping is too costly.

In recent years the homeowner has found himself depending less on the services of the scarce hired gardener than on his own resources. Yet he wants increasingly a garden that is trim and usable for entertainment and outdoor living for all or most of the year. He wants decreasingly the many man hours required to fulfill and maintain his vision. The result has been dependence on the countless new appliances and products offered for ease and efficiency of care. As time goes on, he learns to eliminate the sudden sharp corners in his lawn that add the effort of the bent knee for neat trimming; flowering plants and shrubs are now confined behind mowing strips to eliminate further need for hand trimming. Power mowers and hedge clippers are an answer to the burdens of garden maintenance.

Night lighting has achieved considerable importance of late, and ingenious new techniques and equipment have been developed to create exciting use of the garden after sundown. Thoughtful placing of night lights increases to a great extent the number of beneficial leisure hours in the privacy of one's own garden, which becomes, with the added extremes of intense black and white, a different place.

The garden in America is no different in its early beginnings from all other aspects of the youthful nation; it, too, derived its inspiration and pattern from the ancient design and intent of many countries. From Spain came the elegant, austere, and jewel-like gardens of Moorish palaces and villas; from Japan we now know of the symbolic simplicity of a garden in which each flower and tree has its significance; from England has come the knowledge of techniques, studied for centuries, that produce evenness and quality of design, excellence of flower. So, to a certain extent, no one plans and executes ideas that are solely his. Rather the effort is to test the new against the old, experiment with technique and material, hoping and intending to achieve the personal, the individual, in the increasingly needed privacy of a home frequently sited in the midst of countless others similar or identical to one's own. Expressing this individuality depends on the ideas, the imagination brought to bear upon the vision and needs of the garden in its direct relationship to the house with its aids to better living.

Garden by Douglas Baylis

Chapter 1

A new approach
to garden designing

The modern American garden is less than thirty years old. Before that the garden was conceived as a great picture, enormously expensive to build and maintain, a direct import from cultures and climates vastly different from the American.

This garden was by and for the wealthy only. Middle-class America settled for a vegetable garden, plus dooryard flowers from the five- and ten-cent packets bought through the mail from a Mr. Burpee or a Mr. Vaughan or the Messrs. Stumpp & Walter.

Today all America builds not with the goal of making pretty pictures but with the intention of creating handsome, useful outdoor living space. The garden now is planned as a room, a roofless room, to be used by people. Its purpose is to serve those people.

This is not a new concept of gardening. But in the older cultures only the titled and wealthy were involved. In modern America living outdoors is as much a part of life on the fifty-foot lot as on the many-acre estate.

"Peace and ease" have been called the key qualities of this new type of garden—peace to be yourself, ease in keeping it up. Look at the modern American garden and its peace and ease shine through clearly. Live in this new type garden and you quickly experience them.

On the next pages you see examples of some of the more important variants taken by today's gardens. Their very diversity in the face they present to the camera indicates how personal the garden can be although it fulfills all the basic requirements for outdoor living.

Most of these gardens were designed by professional landscape architects. As a result they usually have more style and often cost less to build than trial and error designing by non-professionals. But it is important that you know what you want. The best gardens come from the joint efforts of a knowing client and a capable professional designer. A thoroughly adequate garden, possibly a superbly handsome one, can come from the homeowner's lone efforts.

Even though the modern house has many kinds of outdoor living space, it does not neglect the old-fashioned, time-tested one—a place under some trees, out on the lawn and away from the house, to catch every bit of breeze. Even in "heat-stroke" weather, when we are content to stay in the air-conditioned indoors most of the day, there are times when we are glad to sit outdoors in the cool of the evening and smell the new-mown hay or the fragrance from a newly sprinkled lawn.

The luster of today's garden isn't only for the custom-built house. Prefab house across the page gains much style and usefulness because it has been well placed on a good piece of land, treated to a quality-site development.

Today buyers of prefabs can require the dealer to include the siting service offered by the prefab company and thus ensure themselves that the original architect who designed the house will have the chance to adapt it to the lot, the trees, the slopes, and the neighboring assets (and defects). The result is a new usefulness beyond that dreamed of for prefabs just a few years ago.

Pace-Setter garden by Marie & Arthur Berger

Garden by Charles Goodman

As there is no substitute for experience, so there is none for the strength and repose gained from direct and daily contact with nature. Modern gardens make this easy, for house and garden are so wedded that enjoyment of the outdoors can be done from indoors all hours of the day—rather than on an hour's tour once a week.

Garden by Farr Landscape Nursery

This is "peace and ease," paved terrace in the shady spot, raised beds of flowers out in the sunny area. Steps are low and broad, inviting to use, pleasing to the eyes. Garden always looks restful, never in need of housekeeping, because it was designed for easy upkeep.

Trees are featured here, but in a way that cuts down on hand-trimming while adding interesting ground pattern. Material inside wooden ring is pine needles, but could be a pretty sand, crushed rock, or vermiculite under deciduous trees. Trellis connecting kitchen and storage room makes house seem bigger, also adds interest to the garden view.

Gardens by Thomas D. Church

Los Angeles, Cal., by Edward Huntsman-Trout

Long Island, N.Y., by Webel & Innocenti
Cleveland, Ohio, by Hannah Champlin

Long Island, N.Y., by Webel & Innocenti   Woodside, Cal., by Thomas D. Church
Framingham, Mass., by Homer K. Dodge   Portland, Oregon, by Florence & Walter Gerke
Old Westbury, N.Y., by Webel & Innocenti   Oyster Bay, N.Y., by Webel & Innocenti

Several decades ago we copied European designs conceived strictly for show, as in this much older garden at the Governor's Palace in colonial Williamsburg (left). Today we consider the house the core, then design the garden as extra living space, roofed in sun and sky instead of boards and shingles. This creates living space that makes the house more spacious, visually from within, actually because of the added living space outside the house walls, as in this mid-Pennsylvania house (right). Sunlight and moving shadows are made an effective part of the furnishings. Walls and fences give it privacy.

Today's garden offers privacy plus a new emphasis on contrasting textures in plants, pavings, and walls. It is close-up beauty, to be seen, touched, smelled, but so exciting to the eyes that it satisfies us emotionally even in winter, when we can only look out at the garden. Dining terraces are deliberately planned for, not left to chance. They are as practical in design as those indoors. Dining outdoors, when easy and convenient, is truly an enjoyable experience for all the family.

Today we make a special effort to create yards and gardens for our children to live and play in. But we plan these areas for easy conversion later into plant beds when the sandbox, "trike" and scooter run, rink and hopscotch court are no longer needed.

Above all we plan for low upkeep. We use open planning, restricting plants to the outer borders so power tools operate efficiently. Plants are in big, telling masses, chosen more often for their leaf colors and textures than for their flower colors. Flowering plants often are too short-lived when we are planning a twelve-month garden. "Color all summer" requires a staff of gardeners, or our full-time attention.

16

How does your garden check on this yard-stick?

Yesterday our gardens . . .
Failed to encourage relaxing: you could see the garden only if you toured through it as you would an art gallery.
Failed to provide extra living space for family from early spring to late fall.
Failed to give privacy to house or yard.
Failed to improve the climate for the house and garden.
Failed to remain attractive through all twelve months without an off season.
Failed to survive summer heat or winter cold unless in the care of a professional gardener.
Failed to provide space for laundry drying, storage of garden equipment and furniture, outdoor toys, and fireplace wood.
Failed to supply screened, off-street parking for automobiles of owners and guests.
Failed to include the needs of children for safe, comfortable play space with sun and shade.
Today our gardens provide all this plus . . .
Garden beauty outside every window.
The beauty of nature, adapted to the scale of the particular house and lot, the local climate, and the owner's skill and the time he has available for gardening.
Complete privacy for sun-bathing, play, relaxing, and entertaining.
A healthful, outdoor sport and hobby for the entire family.
Hidden work center to include space for garden storage and all service activities of running a house.

Garden by Farr Landscape Nursery

A new approach to garden designing

All family activities that go on outdoors get space in garden planning now, with the same standards of beauty and efficiency applied for both adults' and children's areas. Realistically these areas are kept together: children aren't happy for long if separated from "grown-up partying" by more than a light screen, used here as a shadow maker.

Here the family needed a pool house, tucked it under a huge old tree, let the shape of the paving follow the big oval shape of the tree branches.

Where rains are frequent, as for this Oregon farmhouse, pavings become the key to the ground pattern of the garden. But for hot, sunny climates, the paved areas should be kept minimal.

Planting and paving can focus attention on the front door, make it easy for visitors to know where to go. Bumper on paving stops cars, lets you carry hard-surfacing to the door in a single sheet without need for steps.

Strong pattern in the paving transforms an insignificant little area into a handsome walled sitting "room" (right) or open to the lawn and garden (left).

Garden across page by Marie & Arthur Berger
Gardens this page by Thomas D. Church

The eye delights in following lines that lead it on to new discoveries. Skillful use of flowing lines, as here, gives the richness of a big estate to a modest piece of ground.

Straight and zigzag lines hurry the eye along to the termination point, call for an important feature, as this garden house.

Gardens by Thomas D. Church

Pool at upper right takes its shape from a meadow stream in the distance, its plants and rocks from the nearby hills.

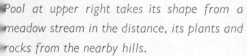

Curving and straight lines, both prominent, have been played together in the terrace garden built not for exhibition but to bring new beauty into daily life of the family.

Gardens are good places to dare to be different with color, as sunken garden at right demonstrates. Full sweep of steps makes grade change pleasant.

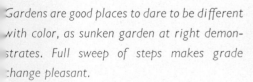

Here the designer took nature's cue: there are no arbitrary elements in this highly sophisticated plan. The sweeping curves of the pool and lawn echo those of the meandering marsh streams of the landscape below it (not shown), while the rock garden reflects stone formations and casual growth found on the hillsides nearby (lower left photo). The transplanted rocks, like their neighbors, are encrusted with yellow lichen that blooms when other flowers are out of season. Even the pool house sets into the slope like a sharp outcropping of flat stone.

Garden by Thomas D. Church

The gardens on these two pages illustrate the modern interest in designing a garden so that people take in the whole scene in one sweeping glance, uninterrupted by any indication of where nature left off and man took over.

This is much more than trying to imitate nature. You must be alert to why nature plants as she does. You must use native materials—the soils, rocks, and colors of the region—as well as native plants. You must be sensitive to the needs of each plant: unless the plant remains healthy, it cannot be beautiful, and plant health comes from all those conditions we lump under the word environment, or ecology, to be more precise.

Widespread interest in ecology is a rather recent occurrence. As long as nature was untamed, we were not comfortable unless definitely in control of our immediate surroundings. These gardens were once not wanted: we wouldn't have been able to enjoy their kind of beauty, nature's beauty. We would have looked but not seen because we couldn't be aware of the whole scene.

Today we take time to see—and we want to know about ecology and what is best for the plants. Not that we garden today to pamper plants: just the reverse. We garden as nature "gardens" because it is the easiest way to have a happy, healthy garden. One result is gardens like these, play space that pleases the soul as much as the body, with a contentment that comes from knowing that everything belongs.

Such garden designing comes not from studying merely the immediate site and its problems but the total scene around the site. The final result is a merging of the man-made parts into the whole scene so that everything becomes one.

Opening up an old house with this new wall of glass made a new kind of garden necessary, a relaxed living with nature.

Here the house was new, built for expert gardeners who wanted to try their hands at creating a lush, almost tropical effect seemingly called for by the way plants grew in this protected, brookside glen. Result is a happy home for plants, a beautiful "room" for living.

Upper Garden by Wendell R. Gilbert
Lower by Thomas D. Church

This living room stretches as far as the eye can see, for the seascape captured so dramatically inevitably draws the eye to the horizon, creating an illusion of limitless space. Transparency like this came only in our time: earlier designers had no great sheets of glass, no good means of double-glazing such great areas. Today we can make any room look two or three times bigger than it is by "borrowing" space from outdoors.

Garden by Thomas D. Church

Here no strong demarcation exists between house and garden. The walk itself invites you to stroll into the garden, or from garden into the house. Yet this is no luxury house, rather a minimum builder house, proving that a fine indoor-outdoor relationship is not a matter of money.

To view the world freely from a room inside is one of the finest gifts of modern architecture and its new use of picture windows. The best solutions allow direct access, as here with sliding glass "walls," permit you to walk out on the slightest impulse to enjoy the sounds and smells of the garden.

The modern terrace is an outdoor room, sometimes roofed, sometimes open to the sky, and occasionally a little of each. This use of grapevines overhead provides handsome shadows and summer shade but lets welcome midwinter sun flood into the indoor living room.

Upper garden by Douglas Baylis
Center by Ned Rucker
Lower by Larry Halprin

Formal or informal, both enjoy adherents today. Often, as here, "informal" lines flow in a strictly formal way, making the old-time separation meaningless in practice.

"Roughing it" at beach and vacation house finds fewer enthusiasts in many areas. Instead good design brings stylish living to the seashore but fewer upkeep demands than before.

The paved terrace must have a good relationship to the house, but no longer do we restrict ourselves to a square immediately adjacent to the house. The terrace now goes where it offers its users the most comfort, which may put it in a back corner of the lot, as in this Boston garden.

Upper & lower right by Thomas D. Church
Left garden by Shurcliff & Shurcliff

This house and its garden look out across a golf course kept far enough away so that passing golfers don't intrude too much on privacy. Plan right and often you can "own" as far as you can see. Why should we shut ourselves off behind high fences and hedges unless there is no view worth trying to save?

City gardens can't be lived in until privacy is assured, achieved here by combining brick, ivy in diamonds, with a hedge on the street side. This 12-by-24 garden is actually the front yard of house.

Existing features often must be integrated into the new garden to keep costs reasonable. Lattice shade here once served as a lath house. Removing its sides made a light, airy play shade.

Gardens by Thomas D. Church

Sun pockets need climate-hardy plants to stand up to the ten degrees to forty degrees extra warmth the sun pocket is designed to create for the comfort of its owners. Alert plantsmen have discovered a sizable list of fine plants in every locality, plants that stay presentable twelve months a year—highly important if the sun pocket is just outside a big window, as in this Oregon garden. Check with a local plantsman before choosing plants for such difficult but crucial growing conditions.

Garden by Thomas D. Church

When the garden occurs just outside the door, immaculate grooming obviously is a necessity. But grooming alone can't provide what you want if plant chosen in the beginning was wrong. Where winters are cold, heavy reliance must go on the evergreens, but only those evergreens that remain happy at the lowest expected temperatures. Where winters are mild, ability to continue production of new leaves for fresh color is of greatest importance. Boldness of leaf, or leaf color, rates high, too.

Left garden by Thomas D. Church
Right by Larry Halprin

Whenever possible, house and garden are put at the same level, making indoor-outdoor living easier. The paved floor is continuous from the sheltered terrace into the sun and shade of the outdoors. Walls become transparent, as here in Missouri, an invitation to look out when the weather prevents you from going out.

Night lighting extends the useful hours, makes a glamorous setting for entertaining elegantly or casually, as you prefer.

Big windows pose new problems in privacy, for often the view extends not into a garden but into the road, hidden here behind screening fence.

Gardens by Thomas D. Church

America has rediscovered the beauty and usefulness of trees, big old trees that may be costly to restore to health. The best gardens start with a tree, big enough to shelter us physically and emotionally, linking us with our surroundings. Today we nestle our buildings under trees, live on a terrace in their shade.

The floor of the terrace may be a wooden one, elevated as a deck, built wherever shade and breeze, view and convenience dictate. House lots previously considered impractical for

Houses on steep slopes gain a feeling of security through broad decks that reach out into the view, bringing the excitement of tree-top branching into the line of vision.

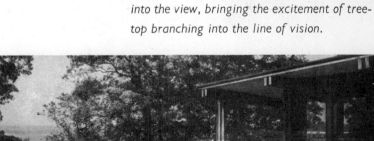

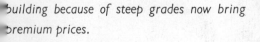
building because of steep grades now bring premium prices.

Designing to suit our lives is probably nowhere better illustrated than in this California garden. The house was old. The new owners have five young boys. A pool house was in order. The new garden took its direction and tone from this. A great circle of paving defines the spread of the sheltering old oak that nearly hides the new pool house.

Designing a garden for people rather than for plants causes us to do many things. We pave big areas because paving dries faster than lawn, so lets people use the garden sooner after a rain or a sprinkling. Paving also can take much more of a beating from furniture legs, high heels, and regular traffic. For chilly-night areas, as here in Northern California, heating coils can be imbedded in the paving. The owners of this garden discovered that they doubled the number of days and evenings they were able to enjoy in the garden when heating was added.

Garden by Thomas D. Church

This new kind of garden-for-living can be created for any existing house provided that there is 1000 to 1500 square feet of available land. If the existing house has no direct connection to the outdoors, one will have to be made to allow for practical operation of the new garden "room." But architectural style of the old house need not hamper your designing of a new garden structure.

Pool house is protected only on the sides exposed to the oncoming breezes. Generous roof overhang helps keep furniture dry. Main house (built in 1920's) shows in background.

Glass skylight over hearth lets light in over fireplace to downlight dramatically the stones of the fireplace and to bring into relief the coarse, handsome masonry.

Pool is often added without thought on how best to marry design of pool and poolhouse.

Concrete paving is designed in squares for ease of placing concrete, to provide expansion joints, and to add strong design lines that visually tie new terrace back to old house. Seat wall doubles as dominant line strengthening this tie-in. Concrete was brushed while still wet to expose the aggregate, hence has little ''shine'' even in such big areas.

Outdoorsy quality of pool house is achieved without sacrificing weather protection of very wide roof overhang, and the use of glass panels in the ceiling.

Garden by Thomas D. Church

New terrace was added to wrap around the old house at the existing floor level. This makes for close intimacy between indoors and out. To lose this closeness would defeat the soundness of the modern garden. Owners here now merely step out through french doors, cross the terrace, go down four steps to the lawn and then to the pool house.

The most useful gardens connect directly to both first and second floors. This may call for adding a new outdoor stairway, as was done here with spiraling large wooden steps.

The garden needs to have many moods. Here is a quiet woodland retreat, left in its natural state to help cut upkeep while serving as home to native woodland ferns and bulbs.

Observant gardeners know that a few modifications of the traditional ways for building houses can open new successes in growing plants. Here there is protection for people from both rain and heat, but ample rain and light for healthy plant growth of the evergreens that bring such beauty to this entrance.

Old-style foundation plantings were a "quick green" to hide a high, exposed foundation. Today the architect avoids building a high foundation wall. We are free to choose only the finest types of plants, use them for their own beauty. In the past this handsome pine, for example, would have been dug and burned by the nursery as unsalable.

Garden by Clarence Prentice

Always we insist upon easy upkeep in modern gardening, beauty through all twelve months for a reasonable cost. All plants must grow a little each year if they are to remain healthy, but today they must not grow too fast because our houses are small and low.

Right: Few gardens provide enough seating for today's extensive partying. Permanent seat wall augments regular terrace furniture here. Dramatic tree against wall is Eucalyptus pulverulenta, pruned imaginatively into tree form from its usual, undistinguished, shrublike mass of little shoots.

This north entrance illustrates the new awareness that "permanent" solutions to site problems pay off in style for the garden. Plants thrive when the correct ones are used for the growing conditions—here lack of light. Traffic area is paved to take wear.

Where growing conditions preclude the beauty of a lawn, we pave, here the whole back yard, now a handsome outdoor room inviting constant use.

Upper & across page by Thomas D. Church
Lower garden by Don Walp

Six years ago this was a graveled motor court. You see it as a twelve-month garden, in spring above and below, in summer at the right, and in fall on the next page. About 350 square feet of flower bed are filled and emptied three times a year to effect this switch, takes one man about half a day each time. Beyond transplanting work, garden requires an hour a day, outdoors spring to fall, in greenhouse in winter.

Garden by Webel & Innocenti

Garden by Webel & Innocenti

Fall relies upon chrysanthemums to keep color going until the freezing weather of winter. Whole garden is only 50 by 50, curls around the house in such a way that it seems to cradle it while also enhancing it. All plants are interesting-looking whether in or out of bloom. Permanent background plants are about as foolproof as possible for the local climate. They were bought in mature sizes, not as insignificant little things without character.

Garden by Webel & Innocenti

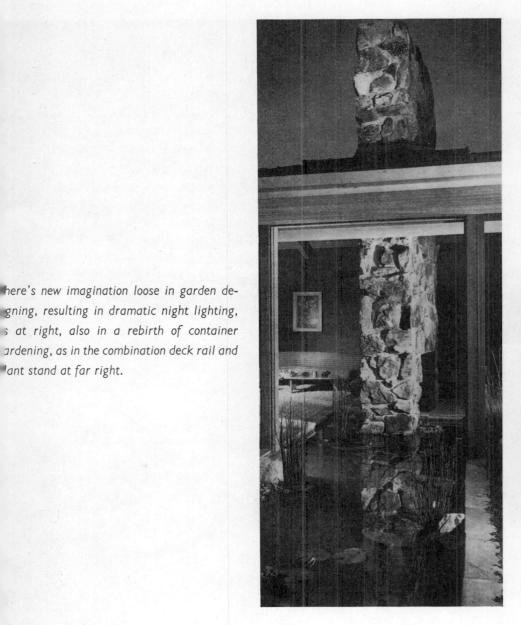

here's new imagination loose in garden de-
gning, resulting in dramatic night lighting,
s at right, also in a rebirth of container
ardening, as in the combination deck rail and
ant stand at far right.

rivacy for a corner-lot garden, here by a
reen fence woven from thin boards. Facing up
 site problems often results in a newness in
esign, sometimes to an unusual handsomeness
s here, a patterned chocolate-brown back-
round for a flower garden decorating the out-
or room.

Upper right by George Hoy
Lower by Vincent Merrill

A new approach to garden designing

Woodside, California.

The parlor has moved outdoors now that the outdoor terrace has grown from a back-yard picnic spot to the glamorous room you show off first to your guests. It fits so naturally today's informal way of living that it has become the most livable, most used room in the house. Thus it affects the way we build both our houses and our gardens.

The paved terrace provides the space and fresh air for holding large parties, permits informal service, which does away with need for extra help. Yet terrace parties can be as distinguished and elegant as an English garden fête.

Reading, Pennsylvania.

Thomas D. Church
Reading, Pa., by Farr Landscape Nursery

Woonsocket, Rhode Island.

Dayton, Ohio.

eattle, Washington.

Woonsocket, Rhode Island.

Woonsocket, Rhode Island.

San Francisco, California.

Woonsocket, R.I., by Homer K. Dodge   Dayton, Ohio, by George Siebenthaler
Seattle, Wash., by Otto Holmdahl   San Francisco, Cal., by Robert Royston

A new approach to garden designing

Terrace living is not just for the new house. New usefulness comes when an imaginative owner sees the possibilities in expanding via a big terrace that can serve as the family and entertainment center nearly all year.

Not all outdoor living rooms need be exposed to capture the view. This West Texas garden turns its view inward to avoid the sweeping winds and their dusts.

Gardens today take on an individual look because they exist to bring usefulness into family living. This may be a place to read the morning paper, or to sun-bathe, or maybe to dine, alone or in party groups, or the need may be for complete privacy from sight and sound for dozing in a hammock. Many charming gardens are simply series of smaller gardens, individual but related in design.

Gardens by Thomas D. Church

Trees can be living sculpture, beauty in green, beauty when leafless. Imaginative pruning is called for, does the tree no harm (left).

Beauty like this comes from good design. Any bricklayer can achieve these results if you supply him a set of drawings. But craftsmanship is no substitute for professional design assistance in garden building.

ight vs. wrong side of the fence no longer xists, for the "structure" side can be the ore beautiful. Always it is interesting, used o create pattern and strong shadows. Decision n whether to make fence plain or exciting de- nds upon mood needed for garden.

he world is our garden, supplying plant re- urces more varied and provocative than ever efore. Modern plastic packing, plus fast air- ne service, makes safe delivery possible from nywhere in the world. But we have passed the nitial stage of interest in plants as rarities: oday they are imported for the contribution ey make to garden design.

A new approach to garden designing

These days we don't attempt to force the land into a level flatness. Rather, we exaggerate differences in elevation and create two-level and three-level gardens that display plants better, provide pleasing lines in summer or winter. But we don't let the lines seem forced. The curves reflect the original contours that existed when we began. Garden shown right and below looks spacious, actually close neighbors exist. Your eyes are kept interested by the flowing curves of the steps and the circle, never really lose interest in the garden.

Angled retaining wall doubles as extra seating space for overflow crowds. Stones dug from site; cap is cut flagstone.

Rough stone boulders, formerly buried at once if found in garden building work, now receive feature attention as indicators of the region. Boulders here merely washed clean, then seated in advantageous positions while the soil beneath them was wet and soft. Unlike rock gardens of the 1930's, today's use of stone limits itself to few rocks, few plants, with each an important, handsome addition to the garden. Black pole is for night lighting system.

Garden by Thomas D. Church

was inevitable that one day the porch and
he terrace would be married. In many cli-
ates the screened porch is a summer neces-
ty—and even for air-conditioned living a
elightful refuge from man-made climate on
hose heavenly days in spring and fall when
othing compares with fresh air. But in spring
nd fall the porch is often too cool to be used
s often as sunny weather bids you to come
utdoors. Then, for the fullest outdoor life, you
eed the terrace.

In many parts of the country the insect
ason continues for three months, but the
utdoor living season can be stretched to seven

months if you employ all possible climate control devices. These include screens, of course.
But screens need not be in the way when not
needed: new types of tension screens, or roll-up
screens, as here, leave everything clear in non-
screen months.

The results are handsome. But, more
important, they have encouraged people to
make porch and terrace continuous, greatly
extending the usefulness of both when much
party-giving brings overflow crowds. The continuous floor also makes easy wheeling for
furniture, food from indoors, and children's
playthings.

Today the homeowner expects the garden
designer to be just as successful in problem-
solving as the architect and decorator indoors.
House and garden are equally important in
daily living. Walls of this living room double
as walls of the garden room.

Garden by Edward Huntsman-Trout

Chapter 2

Gardens work for us

Usefulness is the key that frees garden design. When a garden must fulfill the needs of a specific family, a specific house, and a specific site, its design isn't likely to repeat any other exactly. The resulting freshness characterizes design of all the best gardens today.

Usefulness includes many considerations. Basically we are creating living space, a roofless room. The same human needs for privacy, peace, and quiet prevail, as indoors. In addition there exists a wonderful opportunity to use the garden to temper the extremes of our climate.

Nor can we afford to overlook the spiritual dividends that a good garden can bring into our lives from the close association with growing plants and the miracle of life being enacted before us. Gardens, then, can help us learn how to see, and to learn how to create beauty by the way we combine plant colors, textures, and fragrances.

Such gardens cannot be bought ready-made: They evolve in answer to our needs. We may buy the design services of a professional landscape architect, and it is vital that we do if our budget precludes trial-and-error designing, but we buy his help, not his previously designed plan.

Custom designing permits many far-reaching benefits. Chief is the pleasure of looking out through our big glass walls at a garden that knows no off seasons. Almost as pleasurable is the way the physical barrier against easy in-and-out access has disappeared. Now real unity exists between house and garden, the minimum of steps. This requires much more than simply cutting a door that leads out to a garden.

Such attention to problem-solving inevitably leads to a new look in gardens. But the gardens you see here look different because they were designed as answers to problems, not because someone set out to make them look "different."

Space for play equipment (left) has equal call on designing skill, with handsome play yards as the result. Children like to play in their own yard if it is as enticing as this.

Trike runs laid out in the garden plan save much unnecessary wear on lawn and flowers. Seat walls provide the extra seating, offer no chair-storage problems.

Lower left garden by Floyd Mick
Lower right by Thomas D. Church

When the front yard offers the best spot for the living terrace, today we put it there. We no longer design a picture for those who pass by. And if the garden building is to be a home project, its design is kept simple for home tools, skills.

We demand a floor for the garden equal in serviceability to the floor indoors. Often it is made of the same material. Certainly it must offer the same wearability, the same pleasantness of color and texture. Wheeled equipment must pass freely from one to the other without need for lifting. Chairs and tables must sit firm. Rain water must drain away fast, and the floor must dry quickly for early use after the rain has passed.

Multiple use for all we add is now the goal. Climate control, for example, that tempering of climate extremes, is kept in mind at all times because every change made in garden planning has some effect, good or bad, on the climate. But climate control is achieved as a by-product of the garden design, as in the two examples at the right. Funneling all the air through a narrow opening (top right) speeds the breeze, increasing its cooling power. Shading an exposed wall (bottom right) keeps it from soaking up sun heat. Neither solution looks clinical: rather they become handsome plantings with climate-control functions not apparent to the casual glance.

Upper garden by John Grant

Active gardeners need convenient working conditions. These include ample work space for potting plants, caring for sick plants, storage of garden gear. Often locked compartment is wanted for power mower, garden chemicals, and containers for cut flowers. Add a swimming pool and service needs increase—space for filtering and heating equipment, skimmers, vacuums, and bottled chlorine. Add a greenhouse and there are pots to store, a boiler room, soil and compost storage. The modern garden combines all these needs into a garden work center, sizable and good looking.

Pot-gardening provides quick color, offers an ideal way for the impatient to keep their gardens always in bloom. Can be beds, raised plant beds, or shelves on fencing.

Flower Show garden by California Landscape Society

Dramatic effects transform small spaces into seemingly important gardens. Sweep here is of starkly white crushed limestone. Furniture is chosen with same discrimination exercised for a fine indoor living room. Brick edging does two jobs—adds shadow line to define further a meeting of materials, keeps limestone out of planting.

We pave where grass won't grow, also where heavy use would wear it thin. Where the paving material adds a dominant character, no further edging is needed, as at right.

But when paving is without pattern or real separation from surrounding "floor," using seat wall, as at lower right, defines it.

Both are realistic solutions to this age-old problem in garden building and upkeep.

Mowing strip saves time, defines the lawn. Modern America doesn't have time for hand-trimming, so eliminates the need for it by the way garden is designed. Strip itself adds to decorative pattern and color, even in winter. When mowing is done by power equipment, curves are used instead of corners.

Upper garden by Ann Rarig
Center by Ethelbert Furlong
Lower by Thomas D. Church

New trees shade west wall of glass. Tiny lawn is kept immaculate, seems much bigger than it is because your eye travels out to distant trees out beyond the hidden road. Garden contains few plants, another secret of its apparent spaciousness.

Trellis will soon be completely hidden by its ivy, growing up from the bases of posts. Owner has chosen to "own" all the view to the horizon rather than to screen it off.

Garden by Eckbo, Royston & Williams

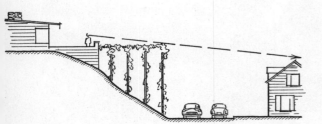

The garden shown on these two pages was once a "useless" scrap of land 10 by 30 feet, falling away rapidly to the road below, overlooking a tall house just across that road. But now both road and house are hidden, even for people standing on edge of lawn up at the new level.

Cost, though, was not prohibitive. The retaining wall is not expensively high, and the trellis, soon to be ivy-covered and so lawn-like in appearance, required only a light pole and frame construction. Seat wall is extension of retaining wall, keeps people from wandering out into ivy.

Presence of nearby neighbors at one end of new garden made it advisable to use light-borrowing but eye-stopping screens of Cel-O-Glas for this little corner garden. Screens also shut out winds, making this a useful sun trap for chill days. All construction here is within ability of the home handy man, or can be custom-done economically.

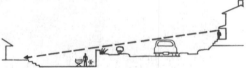

When you dig down for privacy, as here in Seattle, even the front yard can have privacy. Houses sit so close here that little sunshine reaches this garden, hence center paving in white was practical idea. White flowers are main choice for same reason. Openings for steps at each end of garden catch and funnel in welcome summer breezes.

You can't build a fence high enough to screen yourself from two-story houses, but this combination of tall juniper trees for high privacy, brick wall for close-to-the-ground screening, offers a practical solution.

A private world, man-made even to the pool scooped out from what was an insignificant muddy little brook and given imaginative help by its inviting curve of steppingstones, one made for a family that wants to live and entertain by reflecting water.

Pool garden by Edward Huntsman-Trout

Swimming pools introduce many complications
into garden designing because of their size
and bold lines. But their growing acceptance,
even for minimum-size gardens, encourages
us to plan for them as a possible later addition.

Today the terrace must have style, not be
merely a picnic place for "roughing it."
Often this calls for a series of flower shows,

Upper garden by Thomas D. Church
Lower by Paul Williams

ach complete and with all plants in full
oom when moved into place. Leaves with
teresting textures or colors, sometimes with
agrance, are common. So is an interesting
or, and furniture chosen to set the formality
rther.

Why do so few people do anything to
lieve the monotony of a barren expanse of
nd, when, as here, all the visual excitement
color, pattern, and texture could be used?
ants are the natives, but arranged imagin-
ively instead of foursquare.

Gardens by Thomas D. Church

family may want to nestle a quiet,
ceful garden into the native meadow and
s. The results can be handsome and
ctical, a joy to both family and to the one
rged with its upkeep. Photographer stood
he meadow just beyond the clipped grass
he base of the picture. There is no need to
e a lawn so huge you can't take care of it—
no need to forgo the beauty of some lawn,
ing and green.

se-up of open porch looking out toward the
adow shows how effectively sunlight and
dow have been used to make this new
se seem a long-time part of the garden.
bark on soil in foreground makes a good
hion for play by active children. Lupines
poppies brighten the distant meadow
ne, require but little care to stay healthy.

: Sometimes the site and way of life of
arden owner call for a spectacular garden,
e a hilltop swimming pool with redwood
ace, really a deck of planks in duckboard
tern. Trees were pruned into living sculp-
e, come up through deck. Tremendous
wds fit easily into this area for convenient
ertaining.

Garden by Larry Halprin
Pool garden by Thomas D. Church

Even though limited to the space betwe
house and the highway for an outdoor roo
a useful garden is possible, as these fe
photographs at a Seattle home demonstra
Superhighway lies just beyond that fence
only twenty feet from the living room, whe
we are standing. Across the superhighway
a huge aircraft factory. But this gard
remains an oasis of privacy, a room compl
with wonderful plants to delight your eyes

Texture fascinates all who enter a gard
even those who normally think first of flo
color when asked about a garden. Wh
flower color lasts only a short time, really c
a fleeting change in the garden year, textu
of leaves, bark, and rocks offer year-rou
pleasure, a beautiful world that offers sor
thing new to discover each day as sunli
and shadow, growth and the seasons br
changes to each plant.

Garden by Clarence Prentice

Today it is often necessary to provide off-street parking within the garden area. This is a small, street-side slice between the super-highway and the tiny private world enjoyed by the owners of the garden. Visitors enter through the moon gate cut in the board fence, thence between evergreens planted in the path as a baffle to shut off direct view of garden.

None of these rocks happened to land here by chance. But they are indigenous to the area, and they have been piled as they might have been found, so result makes a natural one for Seattle. Plants are those that grow well locally in such a rock pile, upkeep is small, plant growth always healthy. Owners like plants up nearer eye level, another reason they chose to use piled rocks.

Garden by Florence & Walter Gerke

City gardens pose special problems. But you can enjoy privacy, even a country view, when trees and garden walls are used wisely to shut off the unwanted views and sounds of the city. Even the skyline here offers a country look where before it was full of stores, signs, and high chimneys. Wise choice of plants kept the upkeep cost reasonable despite the tough growing conditions faced by any city garden. This is in McMinnville, Oregon.

As for any garden, country- or city-made, the need here was for both green grass and a paved place, trees and shade but colorful flowers, too. High white wall (left photo), catching shadows of the willow, was once a dingy wall of the next-door store. White brick wall, five feet high (right photo), is adjacent to sidewalk of side street on opposite side of house. Picture on the right gives the view owner sees now from his living room. Below right is what he would see if the tree hadn't been placed as it is to improve the skyline and to stop sky glare.

In another age even the city house could have its "front lawn." Today this area must often serve as off-street parking space, except for a small strip skillfully saved here to supply an elegant green carpet, tiny but regal. Close inspection would show city encroaching just beyond the trees in every direction. But at least for this generation it has been kept out by a modern garden designed for daily use. More views on the next page.

Growing conditions in the city rarely are very good, yet in every area a number of trees and shrubs do thrive in adversity. The local garden designers know these from experience.

Flowering dogwood (left), makes a surprisingly sturdy city tree for regions where soils are kind.

Garden by Florence & Walter Gerke

en you rent, the garden must be portable
expendable. This garden could be either.
resting paving pulls eyes down to enjoy its
tures and colors and to forget the skyline
t necessarily must be just whatever
sted because additional trees would take
long to grow. Plantings, kept minimal,
n more abundant and lush than they are
ause of the raised planting beds, in them-
es inexpensive and portable. Big white
a is white sand, edged with tiles set on end,
gned to catch the shadows of a large
ile seen in upper left of photo.

O-Glas windows let light into the service
, transform a high forbidding fence into
ething decorative for garden.

Garden by Imlay & Scott

Chapter 3

Plan for a permanent garden

As houses use glass in greater abundance, their gardens become such a part of daily living that off seasons can't be tolerated. No plant can be a part-time occupant of the view. Each really becomes as important as a piece of furniture or a painting that you live with 365 days a year.

Certainly you must choose each plant carefully, building your garden around woody shrubs. Most must be evergreens. Those that lose their leaves must contribute winter beauty by their branch pattern or color. Avoid the fast growers: too often they shoot up in characterless habits. Slow growers, though, usually twist and turn, take on a bunchy, weathered buffeted look of distinction.

Don't look for exotic plants. Grow the natives and those that revel in the local soils and climates. Their beauty exceeds that of unhappy exotics struggling to survive. Feature the "ordinary" shrub as you would a treasured painting or elegant furniture and gain a new respect for its contribution to beauty.

Certainly you can't start your planning with the bloom on the end of the stalk. Be basic. What does the plant contribute? Weigh its year-round value to you. Consider such qualities as branch pattern, general textural appearance, leaf color and size, possible shadow patterns to be caught on walls and paving, bare branch character and color, leaf response to heat and cold, drouth resistance, and likelihood of wilting. Blossoms and blossom colors then become dividends only, not the end itself in your planning.

None of this means that you ignore the colorful bulbs and garden flowers, of course. You employ them for the contribution they make, but you reappraise them for what they offer. You realize that when out of bloom the garden must still look complete.

If you live where snows fall, take advantage of them. Choose plants for their snow-catching habits. Assign them the eye-catching spots. Junipers, pines, and rhododendrons usually trap more snow than pieris, mountain laurel, or hemlock, but such big differences occur within varieties that you need to inspect the particular plant before you buy your snow-catchers.

In *any* region respect ecology. This science determines which plants thrive together. Soil, wind, sunlight, dryness, or wetness, these affect how happy your plants remain. Wet-soil plants just won't grow happily next to dry-soil kinds. Nor will sun plants succeed where shade plants thrive. Fortunately, acquiring the needed horticultural skill comes easily. You get it by close observation of how different plants grow. Or if you are new at gardening, visit the local nurseryman for advice. But depend only upon *local* observations. Don't try to get by on imported advice.

To get the most, artistically, from the way you combine plants, you doubtlessly will profit from the help of a landscape architect. Building a twelve-month garden is a new art. Few guide rules exist. The old, treasured rules for garden design are no longer adequate. You need the creative skill of an artist at your command. You also need the practical help of his knowledge of where to find key plants.

The garden with no off seasons costs no more to build—and far less to maintain—than the usual and unrewarding foundation planting and summer garden that most people settle for now. The plants are those you already know, probably already grow on your grounds. Only the technique of using them is new.

Garden by Isabella Pendleton

owering trees, especially those native to the
gion, make few demands on the gardener for
me, do provide freely the third-dimension
lift'' that results in shadow-making contrasts
ke these. Trees are Siebold viburnums, *near*
erfection here in full sunlight, on rocky
onnecticut soil (left).

xploiting the natural beauty of rocks and
ebbles brings a year-round distinction to the
arden. Big rocks here were water-worn when
und, ''aged'' quickly in the garden because
ey were moistened regularly with a weak
lution of plant food. Background plantings
e confined predominantly to evergreens.
ring bulbs push up between smaller stones at
ase of big rocks.

eating handsome leaf-texture combinations
m favorite evergreens requires careful
ention in plant selecting but pays off in a
auty that knows no seasonal slump. Big
ves stand out boldly: use sparingly. Too
all leaves make a monotonous area. Sizes
d proportions here are ideal for quarter-acre
, *or a single ''room'' in a larger garden.*

Upper garden by Ethelbert Furlong
Lower by John Yeon

Not every part of the garden must be ever green, of course. But the same care in co trasting big leaves with little, the solid wi the lacy, green with gray, makes for a mo interesting garden during the warm month when your evergreens may look a little d tressed by the heat.

Silhouette a rugged plant against the sky a at once it gains a new stature, often a n beauty. This is just an old stone pine, wis lifted a few feet above the level of the footp that passes it.

...nched foliage against feathery, a trick well ... remember—here ajuga and yew. The most ...autiful, most durable twelve-month gardens ...e the products of designers alert to possible ...nt combinations like this. There is no added ...st to gardening in a creative, stylish way . . . ...ly more pleasure.

...ve a star specimen a good setting and the ...hole garden gains distinction. Make that star ...evergreen, here a mugho pine, and even ...nter ice and snow can't keep you from en-...ving a tidy work of art.

Catch the eyes with bold contrasts—here without benefit of leaves or branches at all, just texture, color, and size of stone.

Reorient your thinking so that you look for opportunities to play bold against subtle, and dark green against light.

Garden by Isabella Pendleton

Many plants will thrive beside a brook. Often you need add only a few choice natives, as was done here—pink azaleas moved from a dry, sunny spot to this more hospitable moist bank of acid soil shaded by giant oaks. Winter scene is "different" but beautiful. (left).

Paving patterns add all-year interest to your garden vistas. Here a contrasting light gray border of bricks confines dark-tone wood blocks handsomely.

Broiling summer days don't bring on a wilted, droopy look to this Dallas, Texas, garden because heat resistance was the standard in choosing its plants. Once you start looking for this type of plant, you will be amazed at the variety available in your area. Not all enjoy equal heat resistance, of course, but on the other hand it is possible to design a garden using only native plants that require no artificial watering no matter how hot the summer.

As more and more activities move into the garden, the size and arrangement of paving become increasingly important. Doors have appeared out of living rooms, dining rooms, bedrooms. Paving to take care of lounging, eating, and recreation follows logically and necessarily for garden to wear well and keep its good looks. Certainly we no longer pave only garden paths.

Interest and variety come from the type of paving material and in the pattern used to lay the chosen material. Your own ingenuity will provide you with many ways to create patterns that express the general design you want for your garden.

A garden pool, even a tiny one, helps make the day seem cooler. Add a needle jet or a fountain and the sound of running water further helps the illusion. So does the crisp edging of clipped English ivy, a plant usually thought of as frost-hardy but that also scorns summer heat that wilts tougher-looking plants.

Upper garden by Thomas D. Church
Center & lower by Marie & Arthur Berger

Make the architectural form dominant in the garden and it carries interest through the months when plants are not colorful. Plants here are in pots, easily and quickly changed to refreshen the scene.

Ground covers are now Everyman's garden material, to be used as freely and creatively as embroidery. They can give your grounds your own design, your own individuality. So used, they give you one of the great garden pleasures —playing with new forms and new patterns, contrasting the different textures of paved terrace, grass, plants, trees, and stone path with the wide range of textures they offer.

Pool gardens, backed up by strong permanent structure, keep their garden look despite the season. Tropical lushness here is deceptive: garden is in Seattle, illustrates what tubbed plants can contribute.

Upper garden by Hannah Champlin
Lower left by E. A. Ferracone
Lower right by John Yeon

Paint your garden with permanent color—from a can of paint. Yellow warms the garden picture by bringing in an illusion of sunshine. Fence above in alternating gray and black is also a vibrant, important element. Solid black area "gains" depth, seems to recede. Yellow is used only in far corner (below left), making garden appear wider. Yellow (below right) makes baffled garden entrance to pool dressing rooms easy to find, inviting. Fence is kept in monotone.

Gardens by Thomas D. Church

Pink and black provide an exciting, though seldom-seen, color combination in gardens. But be careful to use the pink sparingly: it's always eye-stopping. Even a lavish use of gray-leaved plants can't tone down the pink. But with wise use pink is just about the best color to bring out interesting structural details, especially if it can be picked up again in flowers and furniture.

You may need only one small area in a vibrant pink, as was used here. Lively pinks and reds seem especially effective with grays, blacks, and neutral browns. Pinks and reds do fade when exposed to full sunlight, so try to reserve them for protected spots. Don't worry about their becoming unimportant: they carry a long distance, are sure to be seen.

Grass and ground covers contribute importantly to the palette. Areas must be large, calmer in design than need be on vertical elements. Watch carefully the flow of lines, the relation of textures, materials. Colors should not change within one material unless this is a definite part of the over-all design.

For brilliant contrast where you want to direct and hold the eye, use a light color in a pattern against a dark background. But be sure you do want to capture the eye: your light color will always dominate the composition. Keep patterns bold, simple. Strive for great richness in the background colors.

e pot gardener's showcase hides containers
hind its low wall, so eliminates the need for
ncy pots or tubs as each new flower show is
eated from plants already in bloom.

ere's never any winter in a well-designed
rden. The views from indoors can be as
tisfying in January as they are in June. Such
rmanent beauty depends upon architecture
ther than horticulture. Architectural garden
signing produces lasting effects by the use
building materials—pavings, walls, fences,
llises, steps, and masonry borders. These
terials provide a pleasing and permanent
ucture—a skeleton clothed in growing sea-
s with color and flowers, but a skeleton that
o has design beauty in its own right.

Fill the circle beneath a tree with evergreen
ground cover interplanted with spring bulbs
and confined within a ring of paving.

*exture is a fascinating adventure. No place
ffers wider variety for its enjoyment than a
arden. This is beauty.*

What is beauty in a garden?

Your garden must be suitable to your way of life, as well as suitable to your land. It must have a permanent background structure of woody plants, so arranged as to be sympathetic to the land contours and other existing conditions. These woody plants must be chosen for the spots they are to occupy so they will thrive there and also enhance each other as to leaf textures and branch habits. In effect you strive to produce a calculated naturalism. To succeed, you must compose with Nature, using her components as well as she would do.

Once you get this over-all permanent scheme composed properly for your land, then, and only then, are you ready to begin with flowers and color—the icing on the cake. Most gardeners begin here instead of way back at the beginning. This is why, after all their work, their gardens still don't look beautiful.

Proportion is another crucially important ingredient in beauty: proper proportions of lines, sizes, colors, and textures. Good proportion banishes clutter, prevents the distraction of confusion, provides a sympathy of one plant to another. This *is* beauty.

Then there is motion and rhythm. Rhythm can pertain to line, color, sizes, or textures. To be beautiful, a thing of beauty must hold the attention of the eye. The circle has rhythm but it bores the eye by demanding a monotonous repetition that allows no variety or escape. Straight edges on flower beds aren't much better, even at the side of a lawn. It is not easy for the eye to grasp the reason for a straight line. But if there is a reason—a mowing edge strongly defined, a needed path or fence—the eye accepts the straight line for what it is, an honest necessity, therefore a part of beauty.

Sometimes the zigzag can replace the straight line. The eye appreciates the change. Then it has a chance to drop the line, pick it up later.

But flowing curves are best of all. They make the eye sense the previous position of the line, so lead it on with awareness of the planned continuity within the design. This is why planting in flowing groups rather than as individual specimens unifies a garden. Contrast is not sacrificed, for that would be fatal. The garden that is monotonous to the eye bores the mind. Such a garden cannot be beautiful. Loving care and a green thumb can't correct the basic trouble, dullness.

Garden by Edwin T. Wyatt

This is true beauty (left) because these flowers, plants, and rocks occur together like this in Nature. They invite close scrutiny of their textures. They are perfectly proportional to each other, alike enough to make for unity and flowing transition, but different enough to contrast becomingly with each other.

See how much beauty comes from contrasting four interesting textures—pine needles, the notched columbine, tufty santolina, and rough stone. Today's garden must have this close-up beauty. Gardens have moved up close to the house. They are no longer a thing apart to be seen at the end of a long allee or through a vista.

Without contrasts any work of art becomes boring. But a collection of contrasts bores too. So choose contrasts with care—real contrasts like this boldly red cabbage (right), or the crinkle-leafed savoy cabbage (far right).

Garden by Edwin T. Wyatt

This small garden is beautiful because it duplicates the casualness with which Nature combines plants when she builds a garden. A gardener tends to worry so much about the individual plant that he hasn't sufficient perspective to see his garden as a whole. He fails on the score of achieving a harmony of the parts to the whole—or the parts to each other. He fails to see the whole garden because he sees only the bloom on the end of each stem. Beauty does not automatically descend just because there is a collection of well-grown plants in the garden. Such gardens may be fine horticultural exhibitions or botanical collections, but they cannot be called beautiful.

Garden by Ethelbert Furlong

Beauty comes from many things besides th
plants and flowers—over-all design, interestin
contrasts of textures (foliage and structural
exciting shadow play, privacy so the garde
can be lived in, the sounds of running wate
and moving leaves, the smell of fragrar
flowers and rich earth, healthy plants use
rightly and proclaiming their well-being.

Floor runs out into the garden, looks as well
winter as in summer, as do the trees so wise
pruned into living sculpture. Flooring is spl
furring tile set on 2 inches of concrete. Pre
vides handsome, handmade effect for 8 cen
a foot.

Upper garden by Joseph O. Lambert, Jr.

Most gardens start as collections of unrelated plants, simply grow like Topsy. They never achieve the distinction and beauty of this professional blending of plants, rocks, and pebbles because they are not part of an over-all plan that integrates plant material and design.

Good taste is no mystery. It simply means avoiding the grotesque and inappropriate. Your garden must have a pleasing emotional appeal. What pleases does change, of course. This is why tastes change. Today we seek calculated naturalism in gardens. Thirty-five years ago gardening was for show—ostentation for the landed gentry. There were long vistas and allees, clocks and flags in carpet bedding, and the topiary of birds in flight and living plants clipped into geometry. Gardens were a thing apart—to be seen only once in a while.

Today this all seems ridiculous. Carpet bedding and topiary are considered grotesque. Long vistas are impossible, as well as inappropriate on today's small lots. Then, too, we want close-up contemplation of plant groups. The terrace has brought the garden up to the house and into our living room. Today we want to smell the garden. We want to hear the sound of the breezes, the raindrops, and the birds. We want to be able to touch the leaves, maybe taste them. We want to enjoy all the subtle intangibles that gardening implies.

Garden by Ethelbert Furlong

Texture provides the best chance for handsome contrasts. Many gardeners never realize what a variety of textures they have available in plants, soil, rocks, pavings, bark, fences, and walls.

Look at plants. They vary in texture from bold magnificence to exquisite jewelry. Leaves are fuzzy or slick, rough or smooth. They vary in size, abundance, depth of color, even arrangement on the branch. Think of the vast difference in texture provided by plants whose leaves at first glance look so much alike—pine and spruce, maple and elm. Texture effects from leaves are well worth careful planning.

For year-round beauty there must be evergreens. But they needn't be used in the usual way. This is an old yew, espaliered to fit snuggly against its brick wall.

It is not the number or rarity of the plants but the skill used in their staging that counts. This is a rice-paper plant.

Pools can be tiny and shallow, yet they bri[n]g glamour faster than almost anything else y[ou] can do. Every garden needs some water.

The ever-changing pattern of shadows kee[ps] a good garden always fresh and pleasing.

Pace-Setter garden by Ethelbert Furlong

Color, fragrance, and ground pattern—these are well-known elements in garden design. But don't miss the ever-changing drama of what moving sun does to foliage, branches, hues, and structures.

Think how few weeping willows have such a dramatic setting. This small terrace was made just the right size to catch the ''liquid'' shadow of the branches. There is no extra cost for shadow play like this, but your eyes must be alert to see what might be had in your own garden.

Garden by Thomas D. Church

Gardeners are well aware of shadows—but as something to avoid. When shade is deep, plants that must have bright sunshine just won't grow. Non-gardeners, too, tend to shun shadowy places, thinking them dreary, cheerless places. But shadow play supplies a great new dimension for garden design.

Controlled and planned, shadow play offers a wonderful way to make any garden more interesting, without introducing any growth problems and without any cost other than some thought. No outlay. No upkeep. Moreover, your garden will have a freshness and a new look, hour by hour, as the sun travels across the sky. You will gain a sense of change and motion, too—get away from the still-life look—as the breeze makes your plants perform shadow dances.

Simple wooden slats and easy construction here result in handsome shadow play that elevates a garden barbecue into the fine-art class. But a fussy slat pattern or a complicated construction would have led only to an unhappy busyness in shadow pattern.

Upper garden by Thomas D. Church
Lower by Jack McDonnell

Shadows occur whether you plan for them c
not. You may recall some garden that was to
busy because of an unplanned jumble of cris
crossing shadows, some falling on the groun
others caught unexpectedly on walls and gate
Those above were planned.

Children must have shade for summertim
play. This is an artificial tree on the We
Texas plains where real trees are slow to grov

Garden by Thomas D. Church

A structural wall not only provides more privacy than a hedge but in the right hands it can be twice as decorative at half the upkeep.

Here a plain brick wall gets a bold pattern by the simple device of nailing up a checkerboard of wire and encouraging a vine to outline it.

Dominant pattern is carried by the structural material of this fence, gains softness from moving shadows of the Cherokee-rose vine.

Fence above is art as well as boundary because it was designed to exploit play of shadows. Vine is ivy, easily kept trim. Shadows on paving were carefully planned to make whiteness of fence more noticeable when the sun shines fully upon it.

One of the most obvious but least exploited places to get shadow pattern into the garden is via the wall or fence screening the service yard or sandbox.

Fences by Thomas D. Church

Use trees for their design pattern—here a winter view of an old white oak looking like black lace against the sky. Some trees present more pattern value than others, of course. Study each tree for its possibilities (left).

Judicious pruning improves style and pattern. Two-thirds of the trees were removed from a dense thicket, and the balance pruned and thinned. To neglect aesthetic pruning is to lose much of the value of the tree in relation to landscape composition. (right)

A tree placed and pruned to cast shade in summer and shadow pattern in winter can be a year-round asset to a terrace. Even cold climates abound in shrubs and trees with beautiful forms and silhouettes.

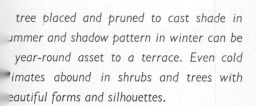

Patterns vary as sunlight and shadows move.

What is beauty in a garden?

You can achieve a vertical pattern from the many-stemmed tree where a single-stemmed tree would split the view unpleasantly. The shorter the view the more effective this design idea because it deepens the perspective.

When your garden is small, obviously you can't achieve garden beauty with the same design tricks used by estate owners who can create long vistas. But your alternative is just as good: you can use rocks and plants in an intimate way. You can see close up the individual character of each, really observe the perfection of their smallest detail and the infinite variety of beauty which the Creator has provided gardeners.

Simplicity of setting can add much drama.

Gardens by Ethelbert Furlong
Step garden by Thomas D. Church

There is nothing theoretical about scale—the visual relationship of each part to every other part and to the design as a whole. If you ignore scale, your garden usually looks dull and uninteresting.

Garden by Alfred B. Parker

Garden by Douglas Baylis

ols (right) please those who prefer formal
fect. Same easily made bowl also serves as
ntainer for a garden flower show. This gar-
n was created for famous Chelsea Show,
ough equally appropriate in design for gar-
n living in the United States, illustrating
w the new American garden has already
ne abroad, and into use.

reflections to double beauty, locating your
so people can see the constantly changing
ections of sky and plants. If your pool is
nly for catching reflections, keep it shallow
line it with lead. Paint a pool black, never
y blue.''

ve for naturalism. You probably demand
crete or metal liners for pools, but keep
m inconspicuous, with the lawn and pool-
plants coming close enough to the water
ide the man-made parts completely.

You may prefer to conceal the way water
to the pool, and have the water enter as
ning water, not as a spray. If there is a
erfall, keep it in scale with the size of the

Be sure plant choices are correct, limited
hose kinds that thrive near water. Then
nge them in the same sequence of their
vth in Nature, from the wettest to the
st soil.

Garden across page by Marian Johnston
Upper right by R. Wallace & Co.
Lower right by Clarence Prentice

Modern gardens can be exciting, stimulating places—or peaceful, quiet, soothing. You make the choice. But for the greatest beauty, don't let house and its garden compete: if the architecture is bold, keep the garden relaxed and a true complement.

Garden by Frank Lloyd Wright

There are no climate barriers to an always-presentable garden. Conifers will keep your garden green, maintaining the illusion of summer warmth and color all year long.

ith evergreens in your garden you can hold to the beauty of spring and still look forward the changing seasons as variations on a eme. When the leaves fall in autumn, a rden designed around evergreens stays in cus. Important trees and shrubs don't lose eir form because their leaves have fallen. ur house doesn't suddenly seem naked in its re setting.

Garden by Douglas Baylis

What is beauty in a garden?

Start with fine plants, display them well, groom and feed regularly. For beauty in a prominent spot prune and shape as needed.

The simple planting often is the most effective, here a magnificent mugho pine with heathers.

The setting plays a key part in the amount of beauty any plant can add to the garden.

Upper garden by Edwin T. Wyatt
Lower left by Florence & Walter Gerke
Lower right by John L. King

There can be no clutter of plants anywhere. Each plant must be chosen and placed because it adds its bit to the beauty of its neighbors and the garden as a whole. Even the pebbles and rocks must not be just any old assortment: they must be chosen for the contribution they make.

Gunnera, darkly dramatic against the natural blond of reed mat used as a screen fence.

Muted pattern of brick wall painted white adds importance to bold leaves and flowers.

Upper garden by Robert Mosher
Lower left by Douglas Baylis
Lower right by Paul J. Peart

What is beauty in a garden?

Garden design, like life, is never static. Today we build gardens as rooms, using them for living rather than show. Like the indoor rooms they are planned for servantless upkeep. Yes, our gardens keep pace with our social history.

Board-and-batten fence of rough-sawn lumber plays up the textural beauty of grassy plants in a deliberately planned dramatic display of sunlight and shadows.

Upper garden by Larry Halprin
Lower by Kathryn I. Stedman

Privacy screens are in demand today, but each can have its own private character.

...lished finish and precise detailing of fence ...mplement a carefully espaliered, fine-...xtured pyracantha.

...erfect harmony in line and color—red-toned ...ax in outsize redwood tub against strip red-...ood.

Upper fences by Eckbo, Royston & Williams
Lower by Osmundson & Staley

What is beauty in a garden?

*Dark paint accents the drama built into th
zigzag board fence. Tracery of leaves of eve
green grape softens effect.*

*Often the simple planting is best—here
mosaic of thyme between paving stones, wit
occasional plants of wooly ears for contrast*

*Good design provides plants with utilitarian
well as decorative value. Pyracantha he
keeps low-angle sun from heating a west wa*

Upper garden by Douglas Baylis
Lower by Osmundson & Staley

Lamps are more than ornaments in the well-designed garden. Lighting ability comes first, looks second. Mount high enough so entire area is illuminated. Care in all details is what makes a garden have real beauty.

A dipping well earns its keep—a great time-saver when filling your watering can, soaking pot plants, or storing cut flowers temporarily. It can double as birdbath.

Tall, spindly plants take on added stature when grown in groups by a sheltering fence or wall.

Dipping pool by Florence Baker

Limit yourself to a few kinds of plants. This avoids fussing with different needs. Hardy wisteria requires no attention. Pot shelf converts a few potted plants into an important, colorful flower show.

Shrubs provide extra flowers without extra work. No matter how severe the winter cold or the summer drouth, you have a choice of work-free shrubs that thrive in your region.

This dooryard planting keeps its good looks all year, bursts into handsome bloom several times a year because of its different plants. Other pool garden (across page) also remains handsome, in or out of bloom.

Upper left garden by Peter Cascio
Lower garden by John Grant

Chapter 5

Flowers without hard work

An impressive display of flowers doesn't depend upon an unlimited labor supply. Most gardeners could triple their present color effect without doing an extra lick of work. The secret is to confine all the high-upkeep flowers to one or two show spots. This makes such a spectacular display of color and bloom that the viewer doesn't realize that only a small part of the garden contains flowers.

This system permits close attention to the needs of the few star performers. The unnoticed background plants fend for themselves. Some actually may be spectacular for a few glorious days each year, but this is not their primary function in the garden design. If you want to grow great armfuls of cut flowers, grow them in a hidden cutting garden in easy-to-care-for rows.

Garden by Edward Huntsman-Trout

Flowers without hard work

New growth on needle-leaf evergreens look
like flowers: choose rugged, twisted specimen
and grow them in good-looking tubs.

Buy and feature at least one fine evergreen
in a really important size. The resulting
flower show will exceed that of a dozen small
shrubs.

Espaliered shrubs—here a young pear tree—
occupy little space, can be counted on for an
annual flower show. Columnar yew is Hick's.

Single hardy primrose looks like a gem in th
setting but would be lost in the convention
perennial border planting.

Highlight a few fine plants

Permanent planting of ornamental grasses contrasts with the all-year colors provided by the fence, seat wall, and the paving.

ou can learn much about displaying a few lants to get a big "flower show" by visiting useums, even from studying the techniques sed for display windows of the leading epartment stores. Clutter is avoided. Backrounds heighten interest in the material to be isplayed, play up to its colors and textures. /hen they can help, accessories are brought , added to the composition. If stands or ontainers are needed, they receive as much ıre and thought as the object to be featured. ngle objects are shown alone, in solitary olendor, or they are massed in impressive g groupings. They never appear in middling, nimportant numbers. All of these ideas have ılue in garden building, as the pictures on ese pages illustrate, especially when you ant "showiness" without much work.

Massing a number of plants dramatizes your favorite. Using small plants in foreground emphasizes scale of the display grouping.

Upper garden by Larry Halprin

Have the trees grown up and shut you in? Have they cut off the view you once enjoyed? Your garden may seem to lack flowers because of this crowding. Reopen the vista, let sunshine and air in, and you'll be able to grow flowers again.

Vista cutting, almost a lost art, once was a hallmark of fine landscape architecture. Few old estates were landscaped without great attention to potential vistas, either views already present, and needing only judicious pruning to expose them, or man-made views planted to create vistas worthy of feature space.

Today's gardens are smaller than those of the past, but vista cutting is just as useful even if it discloses a view only fifty feet long. Sometimes the vista may please your eyes

when it goes actually far beyond your property line. In truth you "possess" the view as far as you can see, no matter what the deed may read.

Cutting a vista calls for skill: no part of garden art is more difficult or more rewarding. Call on an expert for help, preferably a landscape architect to direct the work, a tree expert to execute it.

Center garden by Douglas Baylis

Merge the man-tailored landscaping with the beauty of farm field and distant mountain, as above or below, and enjoy the feel of a big estate for the upkeep cost of a small garden where you have time for flowers.

How often the view of lake or river soon disappears as trees grow up. This was the situation here before the vista was reopened by pruning so wisely done it cannot be detected.

Below, the problem was to get view of water from second-floor balcony. The solution was removal of branches on lower halves of the four oaks. Result is far more interesting than if the oaks had been chopped down.

Upper gardens by Thomas D. Church
Lower left by Wendell R. Gilbert
Lower right by Webel & Innocenti

For a big show at little cost invest in annuals, but remember that annuals create both a high-upkeep and strictly a warm-season flower show. Confine your annuals to narrow beds in front of fences and hedges that have permanently interesting lines. Keep these flower beds far enough away from the house to be inconspicuous when bare in winter.

Flower show of annuals at right has given the Jason garden a reputation for continuous bloom. Truth is that these are the only flowers in the entire acre of garden but no one notices this because the mass color is so striking. This is wise designing. View in left photo shows how hedge continues fence line.

Garden by Thomas D. Church

aised plant beds keep the flower show up
ut of harm from toys and active youngsters.

Couples busy with small children expect the
garden to keep its good looks without making
ig demands on time. This garden, only three
ears old, seems "full of flowers." Actually
ll are on plants in containers, seem more
umerous than they are because they are seen
t close range.

You always save time in gardening if you grow
the right plants. They should have climate
hardiness: it is not enough that they resist
the toughest local winter—they must remain
attractive after summer drouths, beating
rains, and high winds. They must prosper
under the sun or shade conditions that exist.

The plants you choose must have the
correct size and habits of growth. Mistakes
here involve you in hopeless long struggles
with overcrowding, spindly growth, insects,
and diseases favored by the weakened growth.

And why settle for a color display that
lasts only a few days? Modern varieties bloom
for much longer periods than their ancestors.
Many varieties have special ability to withstand
fading in the sun or to hold their flowers so
that they seldom get dirty from mud splashed
during rains. In addition you have a choice of
varieties that can provide new ones coming
into bloom before the earlier ones wane.

You can have, for example, five months of
bloom from modern petunias, four from roses,
three from zinnias, marigolds, iris, tuberous
begonias, tulips, phlox, hardy asters, and
chrysanthemums. From the newer fancy-leaf
caladiums and cannas you can have an
iridescent display of leaves for five months
or more.

ildren's interest in learning to swim and
ults' preference to devote their time to golf
ouse adjoins fairway of golf club) place
ingent limits on gardening but do not
clude a handsome, landscaped look to the
rd.

Growing grass in the shade requires extr
attention to feeding and watering. To avoi
need for pampering, put driest, most shade
areas in a permanently green ground-cove
plant. Cut out slow hand trimming aroun
steps in same way, using ivy, myrtle, c
pachysandra.

If you are spending too much time and energ
taking care of your garden, try the twent
nine proved ways used by other people
eliminate upkeep in gardening. Let your pa
ings flow around your lawn, surrounding it c
all sides so a mowing edge separates the gra
and the flowers that want to sprawl and sprea
Here pattern design of fence in backgrou
also helps keep flower bed presentable eve
when plants are small, offers support f
wind-blown plants

areful landscaping eliminates work and
aves hours of working time. Here's how!

1. Install mowing edges between lawns and
flower or shrub beds.

2. Eliminate hard-to-mow corners and sharp
curves in lawns.

3. Remove isolated shrubs in lawns, or
surround them with gravel and a mowing
strip.

4. Add a garden work center so equipment is
handily stored, easy to find, and in good
condition.

5. Rely on architectural structure to keep
garden handsome even when out of bloom.

6. Use low-upkeep types of fences and walls,
hedges only where their softness contributes to design.

7. Confine vegetables and herbs to raised
beds that make attractive pattern all year.

8. Practice pot gardening to keep a small,
manageable area always colorful.

9. Elevate plant beds to eliminate stooping;
combine them in tiers for more color.

10. Keep espaliered plants enough distance
out from walls to allow painting, or hinge
their supports.

11. Pave lawn areas where foot traffic is heavy.

12. Provide a ramp for wheeled tools and
equipment.

13. Build a fire pit for trash.

14. Use masses of a few kinds of plants, not
assortments.

15. Spray weeds away chemically, best before
sowing seeds.

16. Feed generously to promote heavy growth
and deep roots.

17. Mulch the soil with peat or vermiculite to
retain moisture and discourage weeds.

18. Use the new chemical "edgers" that keep
grass from growing, or use a power edger
to trim around unavoidable lawn obstructions.

19. Rely on power equipment to take work out
of gardening.

20. Buy started seedlings and bulbs (even
roses) in pots.

21. Put seedlings directly into big pots;
dispense with shifting through a series of
small pots.

22. Use a mechanical fertilizer spreader.

23. Use plant ties instead of string when
tying up plants.

24. Keep tools clean and sharp.

25. Use a dipping well for filling watering cans
fast and for dunking potted plants.

26. Let mechanical timers shut off your
sprinklers and hoses.

27. Rely on dusts instead of sprays for pests.

28. Avoid too-close lawn mowing, which leads
to weeds.

29. "Condition" poor soil chemically.

Crushed rock takes care of roof drip (no
gutters here), also provides handsome surfacing for an area often looking poorly kept.
Tubbed plants remain attractive but do
require regular attention for watering.

Water left to run downhill can cause serious
erosion damage to your lawn. Drain system
here eliminates washing, doubles as mowing
edge for upper lawn. Retaining wall offers
seating space that doesn't call for fussy care.

Double-tier your flowers to get more show from fewer plants. Raised beds are easier to care for—less bending for you—and they are good for your plants, too, because of being up out of harm's way. Keep combined bed width less than five feet for easiest working distance. Add a fence behind flowers as a backdrop and to cut wind damage.

Simple fire pit, big enough for the largest fire you should ever have in a garden, makes trash disposal easy and safe.

If you garden on several levels, include ramp for wheeled equipment. Can be mere grassed slope, as here.

The front door should be obvious and easy for visitors to reach. But its very prominence places a demand upon the entrance garden for good looks all year. This simple planting is easily spruced up with pots of flowers for party times, remains green between them.

his garden remains attractive even out of loom because of its built-in work savers— owing edge, raised seat wall, strong ground attern.

Trees in your lawn won't slow up mowing or call for hand trimming if you isolate them in brick-bordered crushed stone like this.

Upper garden by Thomas D. Church

Travel is your garden's best friend. There is scarcely a place where plants grow that can't contribute useful ideas to the observant gardener looking to cut upkeep without sacrificing flowers. You may not rate yourself as an expert garden builder but your handiwork can equal the best if you pay attention to details. Putting a fence atop the low wall makes this sitting area more private and adds the bold line needed to make the flowers in front of it seem important. Everything in this garden, including the apple tree, was moved in just four months before the photograph was made.

Garden by Webel & Innocenti

When a grass path must climb a slope, prevent unsightly erosion and thin grass by inserting steps at intervals. Then you can regrade, reducing angle of slope between steps.

Inserting pattern into paving adds real interest if done skillfully, especially if emphasized subtly by combining with a handsome plant in container of appropriate size.

Mowing strip between lawn and planting makes lawn care easier and directs eye along garden. Set strip at soil level, not grass height. Edge can be concrete, stone, tile, or brick.

Where a ground cover meets a paved area let the plants grow over the junction line to soften it. But prune regularly so plants don't grow too far out of bounds you set.

Big areas of brick are likely to be monotonous unless patterned. Brick wall defines this entrance court, adds its own beauty, as do the shadows of the wisely sited plants.

The fact that wrought iron was often so badly used in the past is no reason to deny yourself the beauty it can bring to your garden. Just insist upon good design, appropriateness.

Gardens by Marie & Arthur Berger

White fence at base of dark foliage saves this small garden from looking overpowered by the background shrubs that give it needed privacy. Loose-growing, carefully trained lilac then can go in front of fence.

Pots of flowers make steps a colorful, more important part of the garden. Contrast of colors between statue and its background evergreens makes both come alive and add pleasantly to visual depth.

Old bricks give a garden an established look. Low wall in foreground is good way to handle transition from grass to gravel. Shrub at right, chosen for its beautiful branch pattern, needed for moving shadows on wall.

Walls offer ideal backgrounds for choice plants but must not be hidden completely if they are to contribute their share to the pattern. All bricks in these Greenbriar gardens salvaged from Charleston, S.C.

Gardens by Webel & Innocenti

Maintenance is relative: you might not care to maintain this garden because for you all shrubs must be carefully manicured at frequent intervals. But for someone else this might be the epitome of low upkeep, a shrub garden left to fend for itself.

o keep gardening a pleasure, not a problem, ou must think ahead. Don't let gardening ecome such a heady experience that you are arried away, only to find later that your arden has become more than you can anage. But, to get a garden you can cope ith, you must be honest with yourself and the esigner. What do you want? What care are ou willing to give regularly?

Steps gain importance if bound on at least one side by low wall. Keeping bricks length-wise in treads also helps, as does neatness in mortaring between bricks. Using the same material for wall and steps gives unity and direction. Overhang on coping makes shadows.

Boxwood of sorts grows everywhere in the South but only a tall plant of this unique shape would do as much for the spot. Such discrimination in choosing just the right plant shows the master's touch in design.

Gates and fences are always worth study, an are not beyond the capability of the hom handy man. Step-down here serves as nature place for first view of garden, a good way add desirable drama.

When you choose small plants, get the flowers nearer eye level by elevating them. Result here is colorful, with no feeling that flowers are an afterthought to the furniture grouping. Urn and table are similar: good idea.

Waves of spring bulbs at base of big tre solve problem of getting color here. By th time tree leaves are big enough to cast to much shade for growing plants, bulbs will t ready for their summer rest.

Gardens by Webel & Innocenti

Successful use of art objects takes real skill. This was blank wall of garage facing terrace until garden designer introduced panel of brick framing bronze bas-relief. V-form vine is pyracantha trained on wire.

Many gardens fail to achieve style not through careless designing but by omission of the finishing professional touches. Each plant, for example, deserves a close look to see which side best fits each view of it in its new home. Unruly branches need to be shortened or cut off. Each plant belongs at the same depth it formerly grew in the soil. A few minutes extra on surfacing a paving can pay off in a new look. Attention to degree of slope and beauty of curve can make a tremendous difference in the final ensemble.

None of these details adds materially to costs. They do control style, though. Next time you visit a good garden, pause to discover the care with which the "finishing" was executed. You'll be a better garden builder for it. Happier, too. Only when the details automatically rate as important can real distinction be expected in the final garden.

Tiny terrace is less than ten feet wide, but prominence of brick pattern in wall makes you forget this. Wall gives privacy but allows needed breezes to reach sitters. Plants are confined to space-saver tubs.

Gardens by Marie & Arthur Berger

Raising the flower bed nearer to eye level of people seated on the terrace makes the flower show seem bigger. But this is design work requiring skill: wall must not be too heavy in scale, plants too dominant. People must not feel smothered. And, to keep raised bed seemingly a planned part of the over-all garden, use the same building material—here brick—for both steps and wall.

Amateurs tend to make steps too steep. Low, broad steps induce a feeling of real luxury and restfulness. If you can arrange steps so that they curve gracefully instead of cutting across path at right angles, they will seem more inviting. Make walking a pleasant experience and the eye sees fewer of the little jobs that need attention.

Upper garden by Webel & Innocenti
Lower by Marie & Arthur Berger

Montague Free, a wise gardener of many years, has said it well: "Do not expect to make a garden that will never require any adjustments. No one can predict the behavior of all the varieties of plants in one garden." And this is especially pertinent: "Do not be in too great a hurry in deciding that a variety is not man enough for the job—some may double their height the second season." He concludes with a warning that many plants must be added with the understanding that they are invasive and may monopolize the garden unless kept under constant check—which means added upkeep.

Upkeep is really what you make it—by what you choose to grow and the demands you place upon your garden. But you do not need to forgo flowers to have low upkeep.

Flow of strong line is always worth striving for, since it gives visual movement that makes a garden more interesting in any season.

For a garden that seems "always in bloom" you must choose just the right plants for the particular spot. Here the key plants are boxwood and yew, the latter espaliered on the brick wall. Neither blooms prominently but both undergo enough color change in their leaves as new ones are added each year that the only other color needed can come from work-free spring bulbs and occasional potted plants.

Gardens by Webel & Innocenti

Chapter 6

Portable gardens

Most people are part-time gardeners who want a full-time garden—one that blooms without interruption from early spring until frost. But few people achieve this goal. There are always a few weeks when the succession of bloom peters out. Flowers are scraggly or nonexistent. The garden has nothing to show but greenery—usually at a crucial time when you want it to look its best.

You don't have to put up with this unpredictable kind of garden. Concentrate on pot gardening and you can be sure of a continuous flower show of exciting color.

In the first place, pot gardening enables you to stage your own flower show. You grow or buy your plants in pots or tubs and move them into the garden as they reach full bloom. Regardless of weather, pests, or unexpected demands on your time you eliminate the lapse of bloom which so often occurs in the conventional garden.

Since the plants grow in pots and not in the ground, you can weed out the scrawny ones and put only the flawless on display. Furthermore, you create your flower picture after the plants bloom, so control the design completely. There is never a dilution of color by masses of past-bloom or still-to-bloom plants.

Naturally pot gardening requires plenty of planning. You must maintain a succession of plants coming into bloom to replace fading performers. The modern garden center is a great help here, offering ready-to-bloom plants so inexpensively that you don't have to bother raising them from seed.

In planning a sequence of bloom you could start with daffodils, tulips, petunias, and chrysanthemums. Another year you might try crocus, daffodils, tulips, petunias, zinnias, and chrysanthemums, for March-through-October bloom. Seasoned gardeners are ready to tackle tubbed flowering shrubs such as camellias, azaleas, roses, pieris, even espaliered apples or pears, dwarf crab apples, or flowering peaches. Anyone can stage at least one gorgeous flower show like this tuberous begonia pot garden.

his luxurious path to the front door actually *sses the service yard—hidden behind the* *anslucent plastic screening that lets light* *rough so dramatically. The begonias were* *own in pots sunk in the soil in rows in a* *dden garden, brought here only when at their* *wer-show best.*

Garden by Robert Stanton

135

Right: Conventional geraniums, grown here in big pots, make an impressive outline for the terrace because of the way they are massed. When past bloom, move others in.

Left: Handsome container like this is big enough to hold sizable pots out of sight, a method that subjects plants to less shock when they are moved from the growing garden.

Portable gardens are a wonderful way to stage bulb shows. These redwood boxes, 6 by 6 by 18 inches, need your richest soil. Bring to the terrace only when flowers look their best.

Trees and shrubs thrive in tubs and big pots, lend a new beauty to the pot garden.

The plants don't have to be exotic to create a spectacular display of bloom. These are ordinary ivy geraniums in pots.

Upper garden by Osmundson & Staley
Center by Thomas D. Church
Lower left by Robert Deering   Lower right by Edward Huntsman-Trout

Be on the watch for big, old containers. These rusty-red Mexican clay pots hold soil and moisture better than usual pot.

No collection of plants looks impressive until grouped interestingly to feature its colors and textures as a unit.

Upper garden by Yoch & Council
Lower right by Thomas D. Church

Pot gardening enables you to pack your terrace with color and still have all the shade you want where you need it most.

Finish the angle where path and fence meet in this way and you have a place to slip potted plants, here a colorful dusty miller.

Make a number of wooden boxes the same size, paint them with copper naphthenate to preserve the wood, use around trees.

A single big container filled with a wonderful flower show may be all you need to make a terrace sing with color.

Or make a pattern as you place the boxes in an orderly way, as in this kitchen herb garden. Six-inch depth of soil is ample.

Upper garden by Osmundson & Staley
Center by Thomas D. Church
Lower right by Manuel Bettencourt
Across page by Marie & Arthur Berger

Use just one kind of flower, massed impressively as a line of color. Set the pots directly on the terrace or slip them into a planter box.

Bon-sai, the living sculpture, can be creat from almost any kind of plant if you have tir and patience. Use them indoors as well as ot Many live for years, get better each year.

Try graduated sizes in three shades of a single color for a stylish, easily moved accent. Collect handsome plant containers as you would assemble a fine collection of vases for cut flowers. Many of the leading furniture designers now are turning their talents to the new field of plant tubs.

Decorating with pot plants is a muc neglected field. This is not strange, becau most of the best growers of pot plants are co firmed horticulturists. They are content enjoy the thrill of flowering a beautiful plar care little about ways to use these plants garden design. Fortunately anyone can b excellent pot plants from these special growers. Show a little interest in owning rea superb plants and you may be allowed to pu chase masterpieces.

Espaliers are always effective. An old technique, but one that requires careful snipping of wayward branches that start to shoot out.

How you use the plants will have to c pend upon your own imagination. The sar successes you have in decorating indoors c be starting places for you. Watch for ways combine textures—and fragrances. Make i pressive masses of color: a "giant" pla made from three small plants always ra more attention than the three as separa units.

A huge plant, overspilling from its p maybe hanging down instead of standing cc ventionally upright, or a plant carefu trained into bon-sai or espalier form can ec for your garden many long memories.

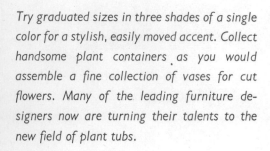

...e up plants grown in tree form to direct ...affic or to mark boundaries. Tree roses, tree ...rysanthemums, even tree marigolds grow ...adily, make spectacular additions to the ...race or path of any garden.

Keep a patriarch growing from year to year to be the one plant that everyone notices. To keep an old plant healthy requires extra fussing with feeding and watering, but the decorative result is worth the effort.

...ll up a few pieces of paving and fill in with ...ur favorite pot plant for close-up enjoyment ...flowers at their best, as in this ice-cream-...air scene.

Many plants have cascade varieties that will clothe a wall in liquid beauty if you grow them in pots for the top of your wall. Or you can grow vines for this display.

Gardener below uses tall-growing pot plants to make a privacy screen that simultaneously displays his skill as an expert gardener.

ould you have pockets in your paving to make isplay space for a few choice plants? They uld be permanent guests, or ones that grow sewhere in pots when not looking their best. he idea is practical for all but the play terrace the strictly formal pattern of paving. But e plant chosen for such use must be worthy, pearl to display.

Luxuriant look of this tiny garden depends upon just a few plants. It can't afford space for out-of-bloom plants, uses pot gardening.

ants in cracks between paving stones must permanent, probably will surprise you by eir luxuriant growth in so little soil.

Pool in garden above provides structural beauty and allows a minimum of expense for plants and upkeep to keep the garden handsome.

Street view of privacy screen shows how completely it cuts off view of terrace garden, which occupies area only 18 by 25 feet.

se tiny dwarfs freely, big mounds sparingly. atter should be able to withstand occasional ot traffic. Big mound here (left) is thyme.

A floating garden calls for surprisingly little upkeep. Plants can be grown in a "nursery" pool elsewhere or bought ready for display. Plants here are mainly water lettuce, with potted ivy on edge of pool.

Pace-Setter garden by Marie & Arthur Berger

Dwarf fruit trees lend themselves to pot gardening, or to espalier growing, as here. Either way they contribute distinctive design details worth the extra care they need.

Garden by Mary D. Cattell

*Take away the plants growing in tubs and pots
and this garden would look less luxuriant. View
above is toward living room (view out from
living room appears across page). At left you
see past pergola to Columbia River.*

Garden by Ruby Esherick

…arden appears to be permanent as seen from …e living room, actually is a pot garden, …anged as often as needed to avoid off …asons. Espaliered pear at right (not same …rden) shows that, no matter how small the …ea, you can enjoy the color, pattern, and …xture of a tree this space-saver way.

Portable gardens

Stack cinder blocks to make a simple plante[r]. The local building-supply dealer offers n[u-] merous sizes and shapes. Cost is low.

Wondering where you'll find space for pot gardening? Here would be an ideal place— brick walls to line solid with great masses of potted plants in bloom, huge old branches for hanging a flower show from above. Really only a pint-size garden until you start looking for these overlooked spaces for pot gardening.

Sun trap below is for sun bather who enjoys delightful surroundings made possible in a small area by pot gardening. Plants also help break the wind, ensure privacy. Because they grow in pots they can be moved to better grow- ing conditions periodically to recover from the hot life in a sun trap.

Flue liner is a versatile material, here bo[th] planter and seat wall. Used without morta[r] heavy enough itself to stay in place.

Handsomely rough-textured cinder blocks cost only 25 to 50 cents each. Colors vary with materials used in their making: these are mauve, which complements brick of the area. You might also find interesting big bricks or tile at the building-supply dealer's.

Look for units that can be combined in a variety of geometric designs. Result can be a new importance as you add shadows and form to rather ordinary pot plants, here an old ficus. Don't overlook chance to cast your own sizes and shapes in cinder blocks. It's easy.

Every garden needs a choice of terraces for the different seasons. But it's not necessary that each be planted and maintained as a flower show. This invitingly shaded terrace is down just a few steps from the main paved area. But all the key plants—in tubs or pots—have been moved to this midsummer terrace.

Paving material here is the round section of heart redwood: the bark and sapwood have been stripped off to lengthen life of the wood. Redwood has a much more summery look than the random ashlar-patterned slate used on main terrace above the steps.

Garden by Thomas D. Church

This is the way a garden can look the day it is planted—if you rely upon pot gardening.

One wonderful plant, preferably both rare and well grown, like this brown-leaved kalanchoe, can make a whole garden "sing."

This redwood tub is big enough to take five rose plants left to grow in the Cloverset or Mennepot cylinders they arrive in from the local garden center or nursery.

Handsome containers made like fine furniture are equally at home on your terrace or indoors but really deserve the better care they receive when out of the rains.

Reserve low, down-lighting for paths, now easy
to do well because of the wide choice in the
mushroom-type fixture available.

Light your garden and you gain many usefu
hours each day. Equipment is simple; wire i:
waterproof cord buried directly in the ground
Underwater lights in pool are built in.

Garden by Larry Halprin

Chapter 7

Night lighting

The best way to light a garden is the natural way—light shining down through the leaves above. Not all the light must shine from above, but all the basic light must "fall," then bounce upward only as a glow from a large surface rather than to shine up from a single point. You want to take away the darkness, not pin-point light.

The staged, theatrical look, so unpleasant in incorrectly lighted gardens, occurs because the lights are placed low, often at ground level and pointed up. The human eye rebels when the world it knows suddenly is turned upside down. The eye becomes distressingly aware that the light is artificial.

The higher the source of light, the better. Ideally, bathe the whole garden from a single source high in the sky, as from the moon. We settle for less, namely numerous "little moons," each twenty feet or more in the air.

To keep the light beam from being conspicuous, use relatively low-wattage lamps. The 150-watt is the biggest one safe to use: combine into twos and threes if you need more light. Always choose the flood lamps, not the spotlights.

Using multiple units also permits you to create overlapping pools of light. This makes it practical to light wide areas without having a great glare in the center. Even a driveway or off-street parking area can become an inviting nighttime entrance with none of the "gas-station glare" you may have encountered in poorly designed garden lighting.

A correctly designed lighted terrace enjoys a moonlight glow so subtle and unobtrusive that if the lights were turned on before dusk, the coming of night would go nearly undetected.

Such lighting requires skill, yes, but mainly trial-and-error testing on the site. You find few skilled specialists in garden lighting. Hiring one speeds up the job. On your own, though, you can do a fine job if you have the patience. You will have to improvise much of the equipment, especially the long shields needed to hide the bright lamp, but every year sees more items available in the garden centers and electric shops.

Most useful for the main lighting is the waterproof "bullet" fixture. The longer its tube, the better. This tube does two big jobs: (1) it shades the lamp, completely hiding it unless you stand directly below and look up, and (2) it confines the light into a cone that forms a well-defined "pool" only sixteen feet across when fixture is twenty feet in the air. When the tube extends twelve inches beyond the face of the lamp the tube can be tilted 15 degrees from true vertical and still hide the lamp.

Ability to tilt fixtures rates importance, since tilting changes the shape of the "pool" from the uninteresting circle to the eye-intriguing ellipse. Varying the shape and size of the ellipse can be used to direct the eyes of the visitor to the front door. Or it can be used to create an interesting zone banding of alternate light and darkness. This produces the visual pleasure of apparent motion, and so a much more interesting garden. The ability to create it rates you an artist. But even less than perfection will supply you with garden lighting which is restful and inviting—and a far more useful garden.

*Light filtering through louvers provides pu[re]
magic for a garden designer to use, also make[s]
the small garden look bigger. Built-in units [in]
the framing of the roof supports lights pa[rtly]
here.*

*Overlapping small pools of light of low inte[n-]
sity alternate with zones of darkness in th[e]
entrance driveway. Makes front door easy [to]
find. Lighted parking area is large but avoi[ds]
glare annoying to drivers.*

*Planting bed between house and parking ar[ea]
gains distinction by its lighting, pleasantly
conspicuous during the day (below), drama[tic]
at night (left below).*

Upper gardens by Marie & Arthur Berger
Lower garden lighting by Thomas Smith Kelly

New glamour for the terrace results from a new use of garden lighting—cones of light coming from almost invisible sources 20 feet in the air. No harsh glare, no exposed bulbs to bother anyone anywhere.

Rocks seem to glow here: light falls unobtrusively from high in the tree nearby.

Pace-Setter garden by Thomas D. Church
Garden lighting by Thomas Smith Kelly

...st arrival should be glamorous, but with-
...sacrificing safety and comfort. Light here
...n garden features: enough bounces from
...se to light for safe footing, doesn't draw
...ue attention to paving.

Garden by Robert Stanton

Glow from house-in-a-garden may be enough
for a dramatic appearance from outdoors, but
to keep the glass from acting as a big black
mirror from indoors you must add as much
light outdoors to keep the glass transparent.

Fine garden lighting is restful. It comes from using many lights, each relatively low in wattage, certainly never over 150 watts. This garden uses 13 overhead lights.

Add ample waterproof outlets while you are wiring for garden lighting: there will be a demand for radio, electric mower, food-preparation equipment, garden duster.

Deep-canister fixtures mounted atop 22-foot flagpole are all but invisible in the garden because painted dull black. Sturdy pole weighs only 16 pounds, relamps easily.

time that light comes from an unexpected
rce your eye is attracted. When the garden
is attractive as here, calling attention so
ctacularly is not out of order.

*Candlelight always makes an enticing addition
to the garden. But experiment with different
heights: small variations lengthen shadows
dramatically.*

*Portable lights quickly enlarge a party area.
Remove conventional spotlight lamp and replace with softer, more pleasant flood lamp.*

Pace-Setter garden by Marie & Arthur Berger
Garden lighting by Ruth Patterson

This rates as one of the best examples of th
relatively new art of garden lighting. Th
house and its garden seem one, just as in da
light hours. You are aware of the results
lighting but not the lights. Only the use are
are lighted, not whole yard.

Line a party area with torches and let t
flames leap and splutter dramatically.

We use so much light indoors now that people often forget the effectiveness of a small light outdoors—a candle, or one of these small modern garden torches.

own-lighting that originates below eye level lls attention to itself, so creates ideal accent hting, also makes a path safe at night without making the surroundings noticeable. Lamp re is 25-watt.

Pace-Setter garden by Marie & Arthur Berger
Garden lighting by Ruth Patterson

Ferns look particularly attractive when night lighted, make useful plants when creating picture for a picture window facing north into heavy shade.

Let the night lighting slant across the wall miniature garden outside your picture wind to keep the night view as full of shadow li as this daytime view.

icture windows are fine if they reveal a pic-
ure you can live with. The owner assured
imself one by building planting bed, here
lled with caladiums, then bathing the garden
ith light for evening pleasure.

our picture window needn't look into your
eighbor's picture window. If you own as little
s 10 feet between you and the property line
ou can build this garden, light it for night
ew.

163

Accent lighting provides the exclamation ma
in garden lighting—here light shining upwa
Highly dramatic results call for simple equ
ment. Even underwater lights can be inexpe
sive.

Light for mosaic on wall shines from unde
water unit. Wall has four units shining
from ground: would have been less insiste
kind of light if two had been top-mounted.

The shadows merit as much attention in the design as the lighted areas. Requires much trial and error placing of the fixtures to get the best shadow effects. Three lights used here.

Light comes from base of birch clump, eye-arresting but pleasant. Lamp is 75-watt white. Colored lamps seldom produce pleasing light in a garden, although the new mercury-vapor lamp can be used for such special effects as a moonlight glow on all the leaves of a big tree outlined against the dark night sky.

Pace-Setter garden by Marie & Arthur Berger
Garden lighting by Ruth Patterson

Chapter 8

Off-street parking

Your own private off-street parking, scientifically tailored to fit modern cars, makes life more pleasant for your family, your guests, and your neighbors. People know where they are supposed to park. They find ample space for the car and for the doors to open. You provide an easy, protected way to get from the car to the front door. Nighttime use poses no problems for the driver. Even party time will be pleasant rather than a parker's nightmare.

But all this requires planning. Dimensions needed are known: see the next page for examples. Don't overlook location—parking belongs between house and street whenever possible. Accept the motorcar as a modern necessity. Take for granted that everyone, from baby-sitter to delivery-man, will arrive by car. To be realistic, provide parking for one car per person.

Select the paving with an eye to durability and good looks. You choose from a wide variety of materials, laid in any pattern, any color combination desired. In order of increasing cost they include gravel, crushed stone, asphalt, concrete, brick, cut stone, and cobbles. No matter which paving you choose, avoid laying it on a steep slope that might lead to runaway cars.

Any paving picks up heat and radiates back at your house, so keep paving away from big windows. Whenever possible, shade the parking area, either with a canopy of vines or by big trees. Properly placed, trees also help channel parking.

Night-light every parking area. Look back to preceding chapter for examples. Be sure lights are hidden, never blind arriving or departing guests, afoot or in their cars.

Garden across page by Thomas D. Church

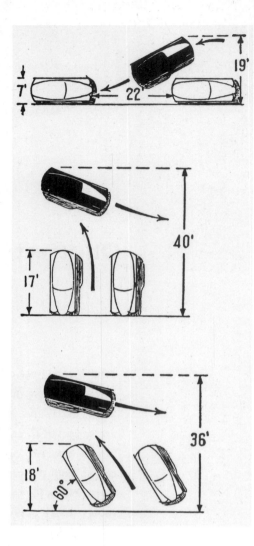

Instead of designing a motor court "to loo_
pretty," try using the dimensions required b_
modern cars. These are the minimums, base_
on expert parking—so don't try shaving ther_
any. If you can possibly afford the space_
allow bigger dimensions.

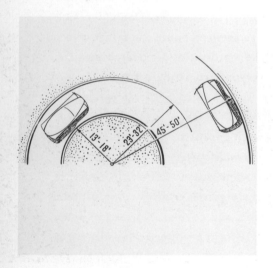

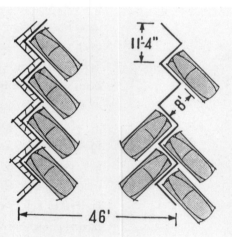

Angle parking cuts down on paving cos_
forces people to park neatly, but does reduc_
number of cars accommodated. Curbs preve_
scraped fenders, smashed shrubs.

Circular turn-around isn't practical today
unless you can spare 50 feet for it—100 feet
if there is to be parking along the circle.

Painting lines on paving helps keep people _
their own spaces, or the markings can be mo_
permanent by making them part of the pavi_
pattern. With car doors getting wide_
consider 8 feet minimum width, best to allo_
10 feet.

Motor court often looks smaller than it is if
you can make it neatly fit an irregular area.
This court provides parking for six big cars.
In addition driveway proper is wide enough
for one line of cars parked parallel. Paving is
asphalt, patterned with strips of granite
blocks laid on concrete base.

This graveled courtyard of generous proportions and disarmingly simple lines handles a
dozen or more cars and still permits easy
through passage. Gravel is sold in various
colors and sizes, makes a much more handsome surface than usual asphalt. Clean gravel
is not dusty, does not track into the house.

Upper garden by Janet Darling
Lower by Frank Lloyd Wright

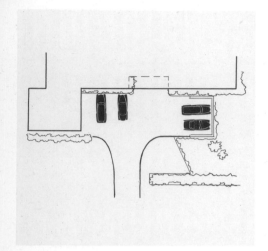

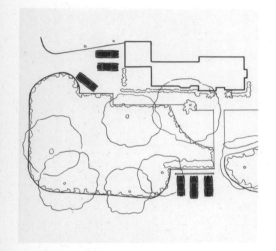

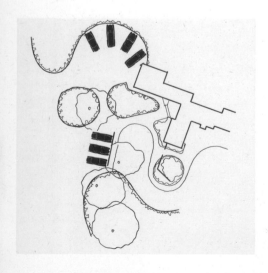

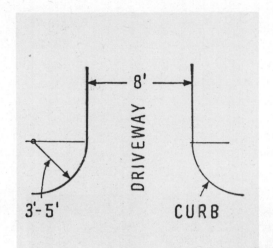

...wner wanted to add both a garage and off-...reet parking in front of the house but without ...crificing much lawn.

These are minimum dimensions for driveway entrance. Be more generous, if you can, to ease turning for your family and friends.

...uests were in habit of leaving their cars in ...riveway, entering house through kitchen. ...ow street-side head-in parking makes clear ...here guests should enter house.

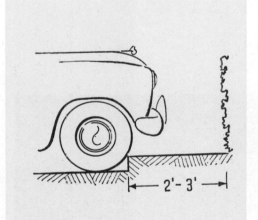

...ivacy-screen planting was saved but re-...ainder of front yard was converted to ...rking space. Requires minimum of 12-foot ...ening for safe visibility in entrance and exit.

Sturdy curbs keep cars off the lawn and out of the shrubs. Tall plantings are held back three feet from the curb to be sure bumpers miss them.

...rking should be close to front door, but if ...u can't add more there, maybe you can ...den driveway into overflow area.

Gardens by Thomas D. Church

Many guests will be driven right into the house garage, so make this as attractive as the front door used by those who enter the house on foot. Louvers here ensure ventilation, also add distinctive style to the garage. Asphalt paving contains beige gravel rolled into it before cooling.

This Pace-Setter House supplies a unique protective cover for both pedestrians and those alighting from their cars, helps direct them unmistakably to the door owner wants them to use. View across page shows how roof overhang extends along past all three parked cars. View left was made from just inside the gate in wall separating parking area from the surprise texture garden just outside the rear front door. A handsome, practical approach also reached easily from the motor arrival court shown in the top photo across page via path parallel and just inside the separation wall.

There's no doubt about where a guest parks or where the front door might be. Overhang extends the width of the three cars, provides protected walk for guests. Plenty of back-out space remains, all without interrupting deliveries or the comings and goings of the family or other guests.

Pace-Setter garden by Marie & Arthur Berger

Garage often serves as foyer today, should be designed and furnished like one, then the arriving visitor knows he stands in an important place—and everyone will be aware of the self-respecting air that discourages the accumulation of junk. The architectural finish, the elegance of the leather bench and the plants, and the strategic location of the garage in the house plan all assure the guest that he arrives formally without any feeling that entry has been by the back door.

ving ''to the door'' is the goal of many
ple, can lead to front-door solutions like
se three, each handsome and practical.

Each provides alternate routes into house, so
entrance serves for both visitor going directly
to living or entertaining areas, and for service.

Adding paved path permits uncrowded, dry-
foot alighting from car, also helps point out
the front door. Brick wall here helps latter.

Upper garden by Thomas D. Church
Lower by Marie & Arthur Berger

Photographer stood on the roof of the house to
show how the laundry yard here became an
asset, a buffer to deaden kitchen noises from
reaching the outdoor dining room. Entrance to
service yard is baffled so that you could walk
right in without seeing clothes on the line.
This laundry yard doubles as a play yard, easy
to supervise from the kitchen window.

Garden by Ned Rucker

Nobody wants to dine among cans and clotheslines, but every garden must have a service yard. Plan off-street parking and service yard simultaneously, and result looks better and is more efficient.

Sometimes the afternoon shade and the summer breezes give the laundry-yard side the most pleasant climate for outdoor dining, a situation that prevailed here. In addition, the kitchen was placed on this same side. Solution practical and good-looking. Big gate in laundry-yard fence allows trucks to drive in when necessary for major garden work, a need important to remember in planning off-street parking and service yards.

Garden by Imlay & Scott

A garden work center, logical offshoot of the service yard and off-street parking, makes gardening more fun for the whole family, even those members who never get closer to the actual digging than to listen to complaints about trying to find the trowel, misplaced pots, or to remember to water the petunia seedlings before 9 A.M.

A good garden work center costs less tha[n] the piecemeal buying gardeners do anyho[w]. Success comes as always from plannin[g] rather than freedom with the checkbook. Y[ou] need lath house, storage space, rainy-d[ay] cover—and privacy.

A garden work center is such a personal affair you can't expect to buy one ready-made. You can buy a knocked-down little house roughly like this, though, and remodel it to fit your desires.

This house now has three divisions—locked tool storage, center for potting, and in effect a greenhouse in one end. The last also holds the family food freezer. While not a true greenhouse—just one end glazed, the roof made solid—it serves well for starting seedlings. In the winter it makes a fine place to store garden furniture. Potting-shed center section of house has roll-up canvas screen (below).

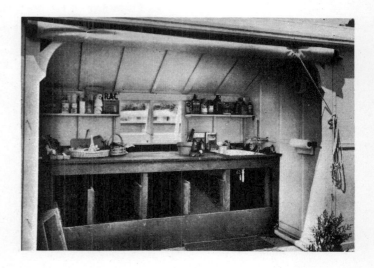

Whether you are an avid or lazy gardener, a garden work center can pay big dividends. As an avid gardener, you get a spot in which to putter at your favorite hobby to your heart's content. If you are a lazy gardener, it simplifies your work, keeps everything handy where you work.

Garden work center by Thomas D. Church

Roofing your work space is important, giving you the protection needed for working in comfort rain or shine.

Make the work center as elaborate or as simple as you want—but make it convenient to the driveway and off-street parking.

Attach the tool shed to the garage unless it is big enough in scale to stand as a building by itself. Simple open-air affair like this may be all you need.

There's nothing conventional about this ya
55 by 125 feet, except its development hou
The garden cost 20 per cent of the price
owner paid for house and lot—but for this
vestment he has made a private world ins
the city. Hidden service yard (above) dec
tively spacious and completely private roof
room for outdoor living, across page, the n
individual front entrance on the street (le
Entrance owes its richness to way drive
widened, dwarf trees added.

Garden by Thomas D. Church

Chapter 9

Individuality

in the housing development

Millions of houses in America are run-of-the-mill, badly in need of imaginative landscaping to upgrade them in looks and usefulness. No one, two, or even two dozen plans, can solve the problems of all houses. A distinguished look, individuality in a crowd of similar houses, comes from facing up to the problems of the site and the use the family wants to make of the yard.

Is there enough shade? Ample privacy? Do you need play space for children? Will you entertain big groups—and where will they park their cars? Do you need storage facilities for firewood, garden tools, or play gear?

Are you an active gardener? Do you have some favorite plant you prefer to grow? Is the soil good enough to grow healthy plants? How is the drainage? Is the micro-climate such that spring frosts will catch your early plants?

Ask yourself questions like these. Let your answers dictate what form the garden should take. The result will be a personal solution to real problems—and a landscape quite unlike any other in the neighborhood.

None of this means that you must work entirely on your own. You do have to decide on *your* answers to the questions. How to arrive at a garden design that meets all the problems then can be a joint venture with a landscape architect. The experience of the expert enables him to cut through to the best solution for your situation.

But isn't all this expensive? Yes, and no. To have a good garden costs money. Barring need for retaining walls or extensive grading, count on 10 per cent of the house cost as minimum, 15 per cent more realistic. These figures assume that you avail yourself of the help of a good landscape architect. If you elect to go it alone, better add an extra 5 per cent to costs to pay for your mistakes in trial-and-error landscaping.

This sum of 10 to 15 per cent represents a sizable

investment, yes. But, wisely spent, this money buys superb living space, a roofless room for outdoor living, at less than a third the cost of roofed space. Even a tiny house can offer the luxury of a huge garden room and a kind of living once available only to kings. The whole family can come to know the delights of living among growing plants, of watching a seed, *their* seed, burst its coat, grow into a beautiful plant. There will be nothing run-of-the-mill about life for such a family, though their house looks like a hundred others in town.

Stylish terrace adds distinction and a new use-fulness, makes the garden much more a part of daily living for all the family.

Design, not plants, provides the key to really good gardening, as the small back yard below illustrates. Circle contains fire pit.

Art in the garden offers a wonderful chance be yourself, to make your garden one apc from the neighbors.

Upper garden by Marie & Arthur Berger
Concrete & iron *objet d'art* by Florence Swift

Garden pools can be any size or shape that best fits the needs of you and the site. The sound and reflections of running water help just about any garden. Costs start at about $75, making a pool seem an extravagance when you are figuring the initial budget and discover the cost of trees and shrubs for the rest of the garden. But don't give up the chance to have running water.

Big blank walls always seem formidable to garden builders. Actually they offer ideal conditions for creating handsome effects like this, here a lemon tree espaliered. Pears, pyracantha, apples, yew, even ivy trained on a wire-grid rate as good choices. Fruiting plants burst into a shower of bloom each spring, bear the biggest, juiciest fruits anyone can grow: the plant's strength goes into fruit instead of the usual hefty branches.

Upper garden by Allen Dalsimer

This house offered no real outdoor play facilities for its children, no terrace for family use. Owners knew they deserved more return from their investment and taxes, undertook a development program geared to their needs and budget.

First step—pave trike and dining space, and a low-cost but stylish arbor for shade. Rely on the grid lines in the paving and the airiness of shelter to create a spaciousness more visual than real. Hide the jumpy roof lines of the house behind the eye-pleasing dentated horizontal line of the new sunshade. Later rest of yard is to be developed for full-time usefulness.

Gardens by Thomas D. Church

...ndistinguished and definitely pinched until ...e small house looked even smaller, this ...use blossomed into the pleasant picture ...low when a knowing landscape architect ...d homeowner got together.

...ithout ripping out any concrete paving— ...tually more was added—and without ...anging the house in any way this transforma- ...n took place. Minimum path and driveway ...e a common problem across America, easy ... solve.

One day a new house may start up in your view, as happened below. Solution was big pines, thickened at their bases by an under- planting of rhododendron.

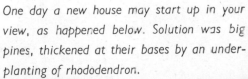

owded city yards at first glance seem to
er little chance for good living outdoors. But
:en the owners who sell and move to the
burbs obtain no better than they could have
eated at the old place.

Owners here decided to stay, hired a
ndscape architect to help them plan so no
tivities would overlap. Result is play space
) completely fenced from passing cars and
ved for easy rolling of wheeled toys, privacy
m street (b) for all without looking for-
lding, full use of the front yard for an out-
or living room (c) for all the family and for
»wing flowers in easy-to-care-for raised
ds, and a handsome front entrance (d) that
ves both the house (at right of steps) and as
direct way into the garden room for guests
terrace parties.

a

c

b

betition of curving lines in path and trike
cle makes this a yard easy to recall with
asure. Further distinction came from saving
tern on usual "back" side of fence as
nplement to rafter pattern overhead. Trike
cle later expected to serve for roller
ting, finally for teen-age dancers.

d

Garden by Osmundson & Staley
Across page by Thomas D. Church

Garden by Thomas D. Church

Left: Flat, treeless at the start, yards in this area desperately needed imaginative garden designing to supply the good living enjoyed at the nearby older houses with the trees. Terrace shape necessarily became man-made, though this freedom was not abused. Result is relaxed and pleasing, not jumpy or shocking. Free form seems logical for the spot, good test of any shape.

Too little space for terrace and flowers? Try pushing the terrace out into the garden. Crushed brick here is held in place by grid of redwood 2 by 4's.

Two scenes below are separated only by a small lawn. Brick on sand serves as both path and terrace. Garden is kept groomed as a living bouquet important in decorating the outdoor living room.

Upper garden by Ned Rucker
Lower by Douglas Baylis

This glamorous back yard was once an ordinary city lot, flat, treeless, small, without character. Out of this its owners created a private kingdom that many a wealthier man might envy.

The house faced the hot Western sun, so this artificial shade tree was built. The ability to face up to the problems of the site leads to clear-cut solutions with fresh beauty and originality like those shown here.

Garden by Thomas D. Church

*Perfect proof that garden building can be art
if you learn to see the possibilities.*

*Fences can be beautiful and useful, here
screening service from living.*

*Terraces give a little house dining space more
handsome than any indoor room.*

*Ample space for growing cut flowers, all be-
hind seat walls and out of harm's way.*

When gardening space is strictly limited, don't waste time on trial-and-error designing or plant selection. Colorful scene across page is a front yard, with the passing traffic just behind the brick screening wall that ensures privacy. Plants are the city-hardy geraniums, grown in pots and moved into place only when in bloom, plus a few broad-leaved evergreens for winter color. Same dependence upon permanent architectural background, a few evergreens, plus potted plants for color repeats in two gardens above. Good rule: use few elements, each the finest of its kind.

False perspective (two views left) creates an illusion of space. Distance from front door to sculpture measures 7 feet, just enough for entrance path between two city houses. Massed pots of flowers provide the only flower show, but so skillful is whole composition that the owners are continually complimented. City flowers must be sprayed or dusted regularly to keep insects and diseases from starting: both spread far more rapidly than imagined in city-weakened plants. Protect new plants from glare off nearby walls and windows for first week.

Upper garden by Ruth May
Lower by Thomas D. Church
Across page by A. W. Hajjar

195

Let doors and windows open onto your prett
view—or create a view worth looking a
none exists. Properly used, even a little p
of land surrounded by close, tall neighbors
take on a woodsy, peaceful look, as in
gardens shown here.

Use every design aid: colorful flowers
served for far end, close to window, or al
sunniest side; trees that experience sh
grow lushly in your city; weekly hosing-of
all foliage to keep it healthy; paving wh
traffic would wear out lawn grass; spo
saving fences instead of hedges for priv
broad-leaved evergreens for winter color.

Lower garden by Natalie G. Bowen

The town house, too, deserves a garden of distinction, as here in downtown New York City. Garden always appears lush and colorful despite city growing conditions. Grass is confined to center of yard, away from sun-stopping fences needed for privacy.

Flowers are grown only on edges of yard, helping illusion of more size to area. Everything kept pruned to allow the most sunlight possible to get in. Paths paved for quick drying and low upkeep—and for strong winter ground pattern pretty even in snow.

Background evergreens are choice specimens. Spring bulbs find growing conditions in the city ideal, can be counted on for great color show if replaced each year with new bulbs. Buy summer flowers already in bloom in pots at the nursery.

Garden by Robertson Ward

The way you solve your service-yard proble
can add great distinction to your garden.
could be from the kind of materials you choo
for tool storage.

Doors of garden house at left look quie
handsome, and they open to disclose a plast
panel ceiling, and brightly enameled pe
forated board, making the structure anyth
but the conventional tool house.

Or distinction could be gained from a n
way of using conventional materials, as acr
page, Douglas-fir plywood, even to the hai
somely arched roof. ''Wings'' increase eff
tiveness of cabaña here as windscreen. Side
house away from pool provides lockable e
gineered garden storage.

All stored service equipment for gardening
longs conveniently out of sight, preferably
compartments to save space, time. Floor
longs at ground level.

Garden work center by John D. Hill

198

sed and locked, garden side presents attrac-
face. V-cut roof rafter is gutter.

Garden furniture, too, needs a convenient
storage place, here in pool side of cabaña.

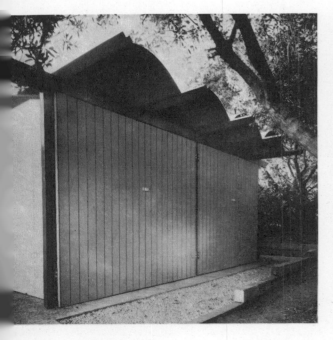

Cabaña by Smith & Williams

When all garden gear is kept in one spot that
also offers real potting space, you have the
dream of every gardener.

When the gardener is an enthusiast, clutter results inevitably unless plans provide for all the needs of a busy gardener. Many small gardens fall down here, with the result that they always look messy and in need of "picking up." Think through your wishes and they will probably call for storage facilities like those shown on these two pages:

* storage at delivery point
* all-weather, locked storage
* no steps, no gates
* sun pocket for cold frames
* potting bench and pot storage
* bins for soil, lime, plant food
* assigned spaces for everything

You are not likely to provide enough storage space unless you list your needs before starting to build. Then plan to use all the space—doors for hanging tools, extra shelves to fit in all the chemicals, still easy to find, bins big enough to hold economy sizes of soil, lime, etc. Provide sectional fronts for bins. If mower is used by yardman, keep it in separate unit with its own key. Keep poisons locked from children.

in storage "walls" here provide space for husiastic gardener, ensure privacy for big race behind them.

Pace-Setter Garden Storage Wall

*You must really know a plant, know its lines
and forms, before you can use it with style.
Mass the wispy kind of plant.*

Garden by Millard Sheets

Chapter 10

Using plants with style

Some of America's finest gardens contain only very ordinary plants. Some of the finest collections of beautiful plants grow in very ordinary gardens not worth a second glance except to a dedicated hunter of rare plants. This difference in results emphasizes again the importance of design: to garden with style, you must keep design in first importance in all your planning.

To be stylish, a garden must use plants so that their forms are well and appropriately displayed—and each plant must be provided the growing conditions under which it thrives. Look at the flowers on these two pages. Try to single out one of them. You can't? They're too wispy? Good! They *are* wispy—so let's use them in big, bold strokes. Let's mass them in strikingly designed, overscaled beds so that their individual weaknesses become part of an over-all strength. This massing duplicates the way the plant grows in its native home, ecology teaches us.

Every plant is unique in some way. You must discover this uniqueness if you are to be able to use the plant with the sureness that leads to a stylish result. This calls for seeing each plant for what it is—and isn't. You must really look at the plant, and this looking must not be clouded by previous knowledge of the plant. Once you see a plant for what it is—as you would see an individual, a spice, a musical theme, an idea—you can use it with distinction and true style.

ee each plant for what it is: then plant to ring out its assets, mask its defects. Encour- ge the beauty of health.

Learn to see when you look and you will come to use tulips like this when you plant your garden. This is gardening with style.

Some people enjoy a glorious tulip show like this, year after year. Other equally good gardeners suffer one disappointment after another—a flower show far from eye-stopping.

Tulips here are of a single variety. They are massed, not stretched out in thin rows. They are planted at random, not in 4-square rows where the failure of a single plant would be immediately prominent.

Bulbs have been tucked back near the rocks so that the rocks seem to rise from the flower bed. Think back on your knowledge of ecology: rocks occur most often when the soil is sandy or gravelly, ideal growing conditions for tulips.

Tree in bloom is dogwood, good companion to tulips because it is bare all winter, letting welcome sunlight reach the tulips daily until now at blooming time, when a little shade from new leaves protects the tulip blossom from early wilting.

To expect a repeat bloom from these bulbs would be to ignore ecology. Tulips must grow in a sunny place to grow fat again after each blooming. Owner here digs and discards bulbs each spring. Garden never lacks stylish bulb show.

Pace-Setter garden by Allen Dalsimer

Quite ordinary garden steps take on a beauty that will be long remembered when the right plant is chosen for the soil, exposure, traffic, and season.

Should the plant be spotlighted alone like a prima donna, or would it contribute more to the garden scene if massed like a great chorus as here?

Creative gardeners know that collections of pebbles and stones can enhance even the small garden when used imaginatively. Exercise your own taste, working the stones into patterns that please your eyes and live gracefully with the rest of the garden.

Try making decorative mosaics from stones set in sand, or add interest to a paving by insetting attractive pebbles, or spread a mulch around trees and shrubs to discourage weeds and keep the soil cool. Collect the pebbles as a family project, or buy coarse screenings from a gravel bank. Or you may prefer crushed bluestone. Whether angled or round and fat as hen's eggs, stones provide a dramatic contrast to the usual soil or ground-cover solution for where grass won't or shouldn't grow.

Upper garden by Harriet Wimmer
Lower left by Geraldine Scott
Lower right by Thomas D. Church

Using plants with style

Mosaic-making offers a challenge to each degree of skill and experience. Start by collecting pebbles of a size and color. Press them into concrete before it stiffens, at least beyond half their depth if yours is a frost area.

Branch out into more intricate designs as experience gives you confidence. Even young children find mosaic-making within their ability. Best for amateurs to mark out the pattern before starting to insert pebbles.

With time even a carpet mosaic like this offers no barrier to home designing and execution. Perfect the design on paper, then transfer it to fresh concrete. To keep within a time budget, plan over-all design in units so only one needs to be done at a time.

River-washed pebbles make good stones, or you can buy marbles and granites in colors. This dramatic floor for a small garden consists of many stripes laid to fit together in radiating star forms. Such a floor might be prohibitively expensive except to the garden owner willing to create it himself.

Mosaic designs by Lockwood DeForest

Make the most of your setting

Grow a plant in a big container and it gains a new importance, makes a big contribution to the garden picture. These concrete tubs can be homemade, cast within concentric sheets of metal, allowed to harden, then the bottom poured.

Horizontal box of rough-sawn redwood is simple container to make—2-inch wood, mitered corners, cleats to elevate box, natural-stain finish. Choose proportions best for plant you expect to grow.

Log-cabin construction using 2 by 4's results in self-decorative tub strong enough to hold soil needed for sizable shrubs or a small tree.

Plant container here replaces usual railing on stair landing. Wood is Western red cedar, legs 1-inch pipe forced into holes bored in bottom planks.

Upper garden by James Fanning & Philip Johnson
Center right by Harriet Wimmer
Lower right by Ted Tyler

209

Despite their bold leaves, caladiums need to be massed for the most stylish result. A single plant is a wispy, floppy thing that makes its viewer feel sorry for it. A mass outlining a path or coloring the ground brightly beneath a shade tree, as before this ivy-decorated wall, is a not-to-be-forgotten sight.

Gardens by Marie & Arthur Berger

Beauty of form in many plants comes from th
pattern of branches or twigs, which therefor
are best enjoyed when silhouetted against sk
or green lawn.

Sophisticated beauty at the right comes fror
deliberate intensifying of a color by adding th
same color: flower and ledge-rock color nov
make even the green leaves have a reflecte
orange cast. Similar principle works for yo
when you choose brightest flowers for full sur
delicate pastels for shaded gardens.

Daylily garden by Bertram Linder

Upper garden by Allen Dalsimer
Lower right by Thomas D. Church
Lower left by Oakland Business Men's Garden Club

ut a blazing azalea Dalsimer between two ray rocks and its color makes a wonderful ddition to the garden. But use it with other zaleas and the color may create a ringing iscord.

by primroses herald spring, but their colors ed the softness of the yellow azalea to tone em to restful pleasantness.

, bold rhododendrons are a joy to own: 't push them back into a border of shrubs give them a star's position.

Separate the colors that fight—and fight they do when you go into some of the bold colors that come with exotics, or after the plant breeder has tampered with the native plants. Think, for example, of rhododendrons. Those native to this country look well together, or bloom at different times, so never cause color clashes. But a wholly different set of rhododendrons comes from an oriental home. Mix the two together and you find some ghastly color combinations. Add the fruits of a plant breeder's labor and frequently you will create anything but a stylish garden.

Separate the colors, easiest by masses of gray foliage, also practicably by green leaves when you use enough of them. Or white flowers can turn the trick. Take a little extra time and you may be able to select other plants whose flowers fall between your clashing ones, bridging the color gap, making the transition pleasing to the eye.

Nor should you forget the principle of isolation, as in the photos on these two pages. Even the most shocking color may add just the right note of style that sets you apart as a truly creative gardener—if you let the entire color show of the moment depend upon the one plant.

Or you can tone down a too vibrant color by growing its possessor in a shaded spot where the weakened light may keep the fullness of color from ever developing, and in any event will not bounce back quite so brilliantly at you.

Also successful, try the graying effect of a mulch of bluestone around an offender, or the blackness of old peat. Visitors may not understand why your garden seems more restful but they will be aware of that extra restfulness.

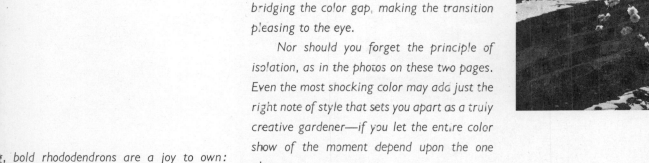

reative gardening can be a wonderful
xperience—and it can start when a child
rst looks closely at a seedling and wonders
>out it. Or it can start when an adult first
oks upon his lawn as one of God's miracles.
hild or adult, great rewards await the inquir-
g mind that seeks to understand the world of
owing plants.

Gardening is a lifetime's learning, with
vs at every step. But don't pack the first
counters with so many things to remember
at discouragement sets in. Remember, too,
at interest wanes quickly unless you get a
ance to put your hands in the soil, plant the
ed, watch it grow through every stage.
ce attuned to what happens in a garden,
ough, you find that everywhere and in
erything you do there will be more plants to
oy, new discoveries as well as old friends.
d your garden will profit, as you put
served ideas to work in it.

Nor will these ideas be confined to plants:
wing conditions and ways to display plants
ter will also be part of your study, with
ults like those on the next six pages, for
imple, where we look closely at garden
ps.

Rugged, broad steps of dressed stone, cut an[d] fitted with craftsmanship, remain reliabl[y] stable, shift little once set.

Discarded railroad ties make a useful set [of] steps for paths used only infrequently. "Trea[d]" is crushed bluestone.

A 6-inch thickness reduces instability c[on]siderably but bedding in concrete is only [a] solution if soil is muddy.

Redwood or cedar slices 6 inches thick [are] easy to handle, appropriate for infor[mal] gardens, inclined to be rather tippy.

Upper garden by Thomas D. Church
Second garden by Osmundson & Staley   Third by Ned Rucker
Lower garden by Eckbo, Royston & Williams

Bricks set in mortar, with slight curve to the treads, test your craftsmanship. Stake a board ½ inch by 4 inches in desired curve, set bricks against it.

Granite slabs outlast most materials. Except for their weight they pose no problems. Make tread 12 inches to 15 inches, riser 4 inches to 6 inches. Tuck rock plants into cool soil crevices left where slabs don't quite fit.

This is poetry in stone, a fabulous background for a rare potted plant—or for a queen to walk into your garden.

Dramatic because planned for shadow-catching, durable because set in concrete. Treads overlap for more finished look.

Upper steps by E. A. Ferracone
Center gardens by Thomas D. Church
Lower steps by Robert Mosher

Garden steps by Thomas D. Church

Steps can fill you with a feeling of warmth and interest, or they can soothe you into a leisurely mood. You may receive a strong emotional appeal—almost like the clasp of a friendly hand.

Native materials always fit the landscape. You can use any native stone, from either fields or streams. River-washed stones here make a handsome, durable flight. Traffic is infrequent enough to make it practical to use these steps as a garden.

Entrance steps need overscaling to give them importance. Motor court is on upper level, visitors come down these steps to the front door. Handsome stepped cheek walls and low pillars have a friendly, solid look, make you completely unaware of a bad site problem.

You can build garden steps in any scale, with wide treads for ample planting pockets, low risers to make a small grade change work like a big one: space is no limitation in the open, and garden scale is much larger than room scale. Make your steps as individual as your garden.

Garden steps can be made—handsomely—from almost anything. Those below were mad *from concrete rubble. Of course you want th* *steps to blend with your house, also to b* *appropriate in texture and weight for the sca* *at which you are building. Brick and stor* *look heavy.*

Garden steps by Thomas D. Church

Have you ever felt like royalty walking down a flight of garden steps that just fit your pace? Or found the whole world opening before you as steps widen into a broad vista of trees and lawn? Then you know that steps can be wonderful—not only set the pattern—they are the garden.

Steps don't have to be broad or long to play an important part in garden design. These offer interesting shadow patterns, and a bold break-through that opens up a sunken garden as effectively as does the long flight at the bottom of the page. Visualize each without steps.

When the site limits you to a few steps because of a gentle slope, make those steps count by giving them a wide radius, as below, where three steps border a spacious fan of terrace. These steps really double as a retaining wall. Garden steps are full of wonderful possibilities.

This garden began when a wind toppled the big oak just as the house was nearing completion. It was seemingly a catastrophe: the owners chose the site because of this particular tree.

The brush was cleared away to expose the main branches, the roots protected by a bulk-head—and the tree left on its side like this, propped up with pipes to prevent further tipping.

This is a far better garden than if the tree
hadn't fallen over, now a low canopy over a
deck in a sea of ivy. Working a deck into a
changing grade is more than most amateurs
should tackle. Call in a landscape architect:
he may simultaneously solve your site problem
and create a new kind of garden because of
those problems.

Garden by Thomas D. Church

View from master bedroom out to new deck and the fallen oak tree, an inviting private world just steps away through a convenient door. Latter is highly important: it is never enough to be able only to look out at a garden. A big wall of glass that invites you outdoors must be fitted with a real exit in order to satisfy most people.

Actual carpentry for a deck like this is no complicated. Owner here followed drawing made by the landscape architect, took hi time, working on and off for three months thoroughly enjoyed the work.

Fallen oak tree wasn't only design problem: house sits close to street and has picture window facing passing traffic. Now short length of fence, rapidly becoming ivy-covered, effectively screens the window without blocking off entrance to the front door.

Mass of ivy, which completely surrounds the house, flows in handsome curves around the new privacy screen, makes the small front yard seem spacious. Ivy needs little upkeep.

Sizable chunk of front yard is paved to provide off-street parking on street side of the new fence. Ground actually slopes sharply from street down to house: doesn't appear to slope because curving line of ivy makes your eye sweep along itself.

Garden by Thomas D. Church

Designing gates is a way to put your person
stamp on your garden, set the whole tone c
the garden beyond.

Simple enough for a home carpenter to buil
but calling for thoughtful care in designing
also in choice of materials.

New materials offer a chance to be different. This is corrugated asbestos board, made into a baffled entrance.

This elegant gate foretells a suave garden beyond, yet gate is only ornament in a simple, crisp privacy wall.

Could your garden profit from handsome gates for its garden side of the service yard—or street and garden sides of drive?

Upper left garden by Thomas D. Church
Lower garden by Paul Frankl

Lower right by Edward Huntsman-Trout

Compare effectiveness of this color-styled garden with the usual spring bulb garden, as at lower left.

Upper garden by Florence & Walter Gerke

...lips and azaleas are not uncommonly found ...bloom at the same time, but seldom are they ...osen with as much care to color styling as ...re. Even the off-white chosen for the fence ...ds its contribution to the effect.

With today's choice of varieties in plants, ...lor matching like this is possible for anyone ...lling to seek it. That the resulting garden ...ll bring new satisfactions goes without ...ving, but, surprisingly, plant growth may be ...ch better: old hands at gardening have often ...ticed that varieties alike in their colors ...em to grow better together than do unlike ...rieties. This is not so strange when you ...collect that the predominant colors of the ...ive plants usually stem from the color of ... soil and rocks of the regions where they ...w best.

...ndering about colors to feature in your ...den? Wash away the soil to expose some of ...native rocks. See what sunlight and shadows ...to these colors. Then look for similar colors, ...d colors complementary to them, among the ...nts that thrive in your area. If you are lucky ...ugh to have the rocks on your own land, use ...m in your garden designing as well as in ...r color planning.

233

Upper left garden by Thomas D. Church
Upper right by Kenneth Beeson

Stretch your imagination and you may come up with fence ideas to stamp a uniqueness on your garden. At far left is bark nailed to a plain wooden fence.

Wooden overlay grid and an espalier planting enrich a high brick wall, make privacy sure but less unfriendly.

Building boards in sheet form go up fast (right), lend themselves to trellis designs for quick, permanent pattern. Winter view remains attractive because of shadows cast by the trellis.

At far left, upended sheets of metal roofing, combined with shadow boxes for pot plants. Vertical lines in fencing and uprights repeat on neighbor's side for his benefit.

Landscaped walls and fences please the whole neighborhood when used to feature fine plants like this pyracantha (left). Choose shrubs that remain evergreen, or those with interesting branch pattern for the view when the leaves fall off.

When a high fence would block off welcome breezes, use louvers. They also let in light. Lid overhead makes this fence seem more the part of a room.

Lower garden by Eckbo, Royston & Williams

Concrete "poured" into a large sheet, troweled smooth and marked into squares, looks easy to do, actually calls for skills and equipment beyond most home craftsmen.

Working in fairly small units, either entirely separate, as below, or as units in a grid-divided paving, is easiest. Big pebbles were pushed into soft mix.

Mix concrete with imagination—and you w never think of it as a simple, dull materi with a gray personality. Add a little imagin tion, perhaps some color and texture, too, ar concrete can become many and beautif things without once trying to be something is not. Its personality is not gray—it nee only to be drawn out.

Exploring the textural possibilities concrete has just begun. You can join in th profitable exploration, for a trifling cost. Use with imagination, concrete can lend yo garden a pleasant new mood—and you interesting experiment.

Concrete need not be obtrusive to beautiful. Certainly its placement should done carefully so that the result is bo interesting and artful. Texture depends both materials used and the finish applied. does color, or at least the apparent color, f smooth, troweled finishes always make a m look lighter in color than rough finishes.

These four pages can introduce you only a few possibilities in what you can do.

Lower garden by Eckbo, Royston & Williams

Problem here was to create a quick, low-cost
way to enrich a small new house. Great style
was achieved by imaginative use of big circles
of concrete, repeating circle of carpet indoors.

Upper garden by Eckbo, Royston & Williams

Wheelbarrow offers space enough for mixing about as much concrete as you can conveniently use while in its best physical condition—unless you are paving a big area. In that event have a ready-mix truck deliver your needs ready to go in your forms. Where once you had to home-mix sand, gravel, and cement for small batches you can now buy Sakrete and just add water to bring it to a workable state.

Rough troweling, above, makes for a non-skid surface, less glare, more work in sweeping or washing. Usual tool to produce rough finish is the wood float.

For hard, smooth surface follow wood floating with steel-troweling, right above. Surface then has great wearing ability, even under traffic. But it is slippery and reflective.

To avoid prominent cracking, pattern can be applied before concrete sets. Then cracks will occur in the pattern grid if ground settles. Tool being used is a groover.

You are not restricted to applied patterns when you use concrete, even for paving. Here are drain tiles, a saucer for a flowerpot, pieces of asbestos pipe, strips of corrugated and flat asbestos board, and a half brick. They represent materials that can be sectioned and finished flush to create texture design. Circular materials may enclose concrete of different color, as for a polka-dot floor for a play yard. Corrugated asbestos board, as used at right, sometimes can be picked up without cost as waste at dealers.

Decorative pattern, produced with an ordin[ary] cooky cutter, illustrates just one of many g[ood] non-slip finishes logical to use. Once y[ou] understand the nature of concrete, you can [do] dozens of interesting ways to get a uniq[ue] pattern for your garden.

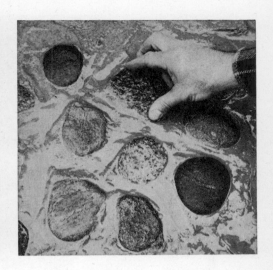

Make exposed-aggregate concrete by scrubbing away the cement and sand paste after the slab has set hard enough to support weight without denting. Fiber broom, fiber brush, and plenty of water will do the job. But wash stones clean: only acid cleans them once concrete sets.

Pebbles pressed into the still-soft surface stretch a limited supply of colored material, but result is not as winter-hardy as true exposed aggregate. Using big rocks, though, as at upper right, is satisfactory. Roughening surface by stiff-brooming is a compromise where effort required for exposing aggregate seems too great. All of these treatments make the paving somewhat harder to keep clean, but do introduce handsome textures.

You can let the surrounding soil be your form when making isolated pieces of any shape. Simply tamp the soil firm, trace out on it your design, dig down neatly, place your concrete mix in the resulting "form." Only problem you may run into is a mixing of the soil with the concrete if the latter is too wet when dumped into hole. Mixing in soil weakens the concrete.

Complicated designs take time to create but offer no real problem to the determined amateur with available time. Choose chips of known weather resistance. To get them bedded firmly, use a kitchen rolling pin.

Notched 2 by 4's show a method of joining grid dividers used to obtain paving effect shown at the right. Dividers remain in place, last ten years or more if redwood, can be stained to make pattern more distinct.

Skytex windshield converts this small garden into a comfortable sun-trap room.

Garden by Eckbo, Royston & Williams

Chapter 11

Climate control

Are you missing a lot of good outdoor living because you can be comfortable in your garden only for a few weeks a year? Many homeowners are in this predicament. Yet by exercising just a little ingenuity you can easily take the sting out of spring and fall, the sweltering out of humid midsummer.

This kind of climate control is neither difficult nor expensive. You manipulate the walls, fences, and hedges you would buy anyhow for privacy, the pavings you put down for safe, dry footing, the roof overhangs; you build for good looks; the plants you grow for color in your garden. How you combine all these depends upon your climate problems.

You can't do anything about the over-all climate of your community, of course. You *can* fix the climate in your own yard. No single change alters the climate drastically, but each helps. The sum total makes an impressive change. Your private climate can be as much as forty degrees warmer in marginal weather, ten degrees cooler in hot weather, simply because you follow the proven ways to manipulate it.

Your comfort outdoors depends not so much on air temperature as on whether you are 1) in direct sun, 2) in a breeze. You can be quite comfortable on a chilly day as long as you stay in the sun and are protected from wind. On a hot day you can be more comfortable in the sun and breeze than in the shade without breeze, though the air temperature is no different.

Recall, too, that glare is dangerously bouncing at you not only light that annoys your eyes but radiant heat. You can feel the latter if you sit by an open window in summer: you will feel the hot pavement or the wall of the house next door as a glow on your face, a tree as coolness on your face. Have a *tall* tree close to your house to cut off this sky glare.

here's no shut-in feeling because the light nters freely, also because framing is kept in, furniture uncrowded. Remove screens in idsummer.

241

If you live in a climate where the nights are usually cool, even though the days are sunny and warm, put up sky shades that can be pulled across at dusk to imprison the heat absorbed by the paving. Otherwise the heat reradiates up into the super-chilled night sky and is lost.

If you live where too bright light is the problem, rely upon screen like that of bamboo poles, below, while you wait for trees to grow. Then your garden will be immediately livable.

Upper garden by Thomas D. Church
Lower left by Osmundson & Staley
Lower right by E. A. Ferracone

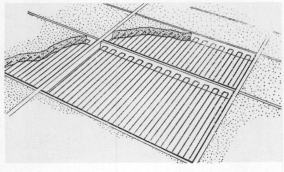

Below: Let nothing interfere with the prevailing summer breeze. Enjoy your privacy, yes, but by louver fences where solid ones would cut off the breezes. Actually louver fences protect bigger areas than do solid walls: the wind is slowed, not stopped, true, but any time you manage to stop wind you pay for the small calm spot by having beyond it an area of shifting, sudden, annoying gusts and whirls. Then sand gets sucked up, dead leaves swirl around, and old newspapers mysteriously appear and join the dance. You don't really stop the wind: you merely make it vicious. Louver fences avoid this hazard.

Radiant heat, from an electric system (above), akes the chill out of the evening, greatly expanding the usefulness of your terrace. Users all the cost a good investment, offset by the avings in wear and tear on the house.

Fire pit operates from gas line, uses green wood that lasts a long time. It is more psychological than functional in heating.

Gardens by Thomas D. Church

Man-made sun stopper provides effective shade while you wait for new trees to grow big enough to do the job. Open space between fence and roof siphons off rising warm air.

Both privacy and climate control should start at your lot line. This double-duty fence of standard building blocks—upper blocks turned on edge—provides privacy while admitting the welcome breezes.

Upper garden by Don Hannistrom
Lower by Eckbo, Royston & Williams

low: When shade tree is directly west of the
reened porch you enjoy morning sun for
eakfast on the porch or under the tree. By
nch time the tree completely shades the
rrace. As the sun moves around, the tree
eps deadly afternoon-sun heat off the west
all of your house.

Below: A vertical-louver fence converts a small
corner of the garden into an outdoor dining
room, complete with ventilation and without
danger of creating a heat trap.

arden house may be much more practical for
cal climate if built without permanent side
alls to cut off the cooling breezes. Simple
ambco screens, shown rolled here, provide
te afternoon-sun screening.

Upper left garden by Farr Landscape Nursery
Upper right by W. A. Huebsch

Climate control

Children need shade as well as sun to play in
Lightweight structural steel makes a useful
material for building a handsome playground
shade. Canopy is of wood slats 1 by 2 inches
set on edge. Later trees will tower above sun
shade and make area have a more intimate
look.

You can have an outdoor cooling system in hot
weather if you slowly wet a masonry surface,
let it cool you by radiant cooling as the water
evaporates into the air.

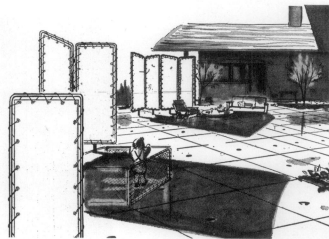

Screens of laced canvas slip into metal sockets
countersunk in the terrace like the flag on a
golf green, provide easy way to enjoy movable
protection from hot sun or chilling wind as
each need arises.

Garden by Thomas D. Church

Protect against frost by draining off the frosty air that accumulates close to the ground on cold nights. This air behaves like sluggish water, flowing downhill if it has a chance. Open gate on low side to let it escape downhill.

Avoid frost-collecting pockets at the bottoms of slopes when choosing homes for frost-shy plants. Those growing a few feet up the slope often escape chilling air flow.

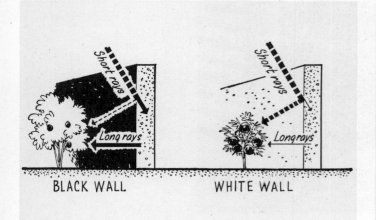

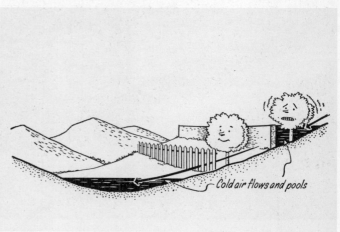

Sun heat arrives as short-wave rays. Black wall soaks up most of these, leaving little direct daytime reflection but much day and night radiant heating by long-wave rays. Both long and short rays stimulate growth.

Solid wall upslope protects your garden from frost that might flow downhill from your neighbor's garden. But leave opening in your downhill fence. Keep necessary obstructions minimal: air flow is weak.

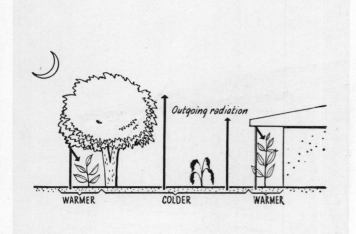

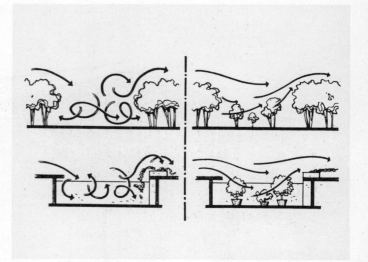

Soil and plants chill quickly on clear night by direct radiation of heat to the subzero stratosphere unless something opaque prevents this. Air temperature unchanged but plant escapes.

Presence of trees in clearing tends to smooth gusts into gentle, even breezes. Potted shrubs on an enclosed patio may eliminate turbulence, drafts, and faulty operation of barbecue.

Adding a garden room for summer shade may also lead to ideal growing conditions for tender plants that then can be enjoyed more fully in close-up viewing. Heavy, rough lumber and the imaginative inside-out construction make this lath house extra handsome.

A cool, breezy garden work center make warm-weather tasks a pleasure. Lath scree. shading work area is omitted from front half o shed to make more airy the garden sittin, room. Combining two little units into one bi, one helps keep a garden from looking cluttered

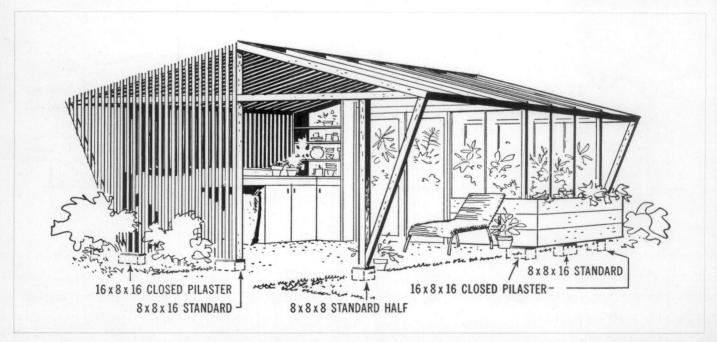

16 x 8 x 16 CLOSED PILASTER
8 x 8 x 16 STANDARD

8 x 8 x 8 STANDARD HALF

16 x 8 x 16 CLOSED PILASTER

8 x 8 x 16 STANDARD

Upper garden house by Harry W. Shepherd
Lower by Leavitt Dudley

When you don't have enough roof overhang to shade south and west walls, you can stretch your protection by adding a vine-covered trellis: Choose a kind of plant that loses its leaves in winter and you enjoy ample light all winter, shade right when you need it most.

You can't keep out the sun of late, late afternoon no matter how big your trellis, of course, but you will keep its scorch from soaking into the paving and annoying you later in the evening as a "radiator." The only shield against low sun is something vertical and tall.

Keep paving colors in the middle tones—neither glaring nor excessively heat-absorbing. When you possibly can, add trees to shade the paving from direct sun part of the day. Try to stick to greens and grays in plants, avoiding hot flower colors.

Upper garden by Larry Halprin
Lower garden by Eckbo, Royston & Williams

This little green oasis offers eloquent testimony to climate control: the surrounding country was parched and browned on the 105° July day the photograph was made.

…anning supplied the key to the coolness built …to this house and the lush growth possible in … inside garden. The house is not mechanically …-conditioned—and no amount of watering …uld make caladium, fern, dicentra, alocasia, …, and ginger do well if other conditions were …t also right.

A whole bagful of aerodynamic ideas …nt into the design. But bringing the garden …doors and creating a hole in the roof for a …imneylike action to suck heat out and cooler … from near the ground into the house are the … ones. Roof opening is screened, keeping out …ects and breaking rain into smaller drops. … snow country it probably would be replaced … a skylight in the winter.

Chimney action now sets up an air flow …n on days of absolute calm. Complete open- …s of house—dining room (upper right) and …ng room (lower right) are separated only by … screen wall in summer, sliding glass doors …winter—assures that air flow will draw heat … of all living areas. Only the north and west …lls of house have small windows, ample to …w pleasant southwest breeze of summer to …ape but small enough to avoid inviting bad …ter winds.

House & garden by Richard A. Kuhlman

Climate control

When you seek both shade and wind protection, Indian teepee offers easiest form to erect, self-supporting from its rafters 2 by 6 inches. This house measures 20 feet long, accommodates 12 people in comfort, could be lengthened readily to seat 18. If you are in rainy area, partially close open end. If flies or mosquitoes are a local problem, substitute tension screens for doors.

When you need only shade, quick solution is canvas laced to simple post-and-beam frame.

Upper garden by John Carmack
Lower by Osmundson & Staley

ite triangles are made of canvas, other
ngles and entire roof are of Vimlite, a
e-reinforced plastic. Or you could buy
nite or a similar corrugated plastic panel-

ating your shelter on a wooden deck en-
s against flooding during heavy rains, also
people high enough so they avoid worrying
t sitting too close to chilly, damp ground.

Climate control

Don't suffer through another summer of oppressive heat. Plant trees, shrubs, and vines in the right locations to keep you comfortable. Big tree here was moved in previous winter.

Afternoon sun is the "killer." You must keep it off your house or suffer all night as the soaked-up heat reradiates at you. High tree protects roof in early afternoon, hedge takes over against late sun.

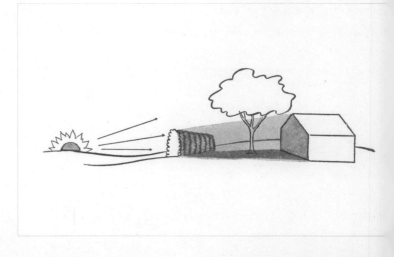

It's no trick for a professional to move a big shade tree. All these trees were planted only six months before the photograph was made. The cost of enjoying abundant shade at once? About $400 to $600 for tree 20 feet to 30 feet.

If you can't find a big tree for sale, use three smaller ones, planted as a clump or in a row. Reliable nurseries guarantee that trees they plant will survive moving.

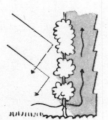

Vines, nature's shade maker, easily convert into a highly decorative addition to garden. Choose deciduous types and the winter sun will warm the wall, help cut your heating bill. Plant vines 6 inches from wall.

For humid days: Graveled terrace 3 ste
above the manicured little garden expo:
people to any chance breezes for days wh
any air movement would be welcome. Sa
terrace serves spring and fall, too, expos
people to full sun heat on calm days, chilly
sunny.

Garden by Ned Rucker

For windy days: Many times you need only the protection of a glass windshield, fence, or hedge. Shelter house here offers additional protection, also shade, fireplace heat, and a rainy-day cover overhead.

Cantilevered sunshade takes over where natural tree shade stops. Roof angles up, making structure seem bigger and more impressive. Attaches to any existing building or fence.

257

"Privacy . . . the right to be alone—the most comprehensive of rights—the right most valued by civilized men."

Louis D. Brandeis
Justice United States Supreme Court

Privacy

Good living is not public living. Your whole property, garden as well as house, should permit you to relax. But you can't relax if you must remain on view and dress parade because the world is looking over your shoulder. Securing the freedom of privacy is usually surprisingly simple, sometimes as simple as putting up a good-looking fence.

If your neighbors can observe what you are serving on your terrace, your home is not really your castle. If you can't walk into the garden from your bedroom to pick a flower before breakfast without being seen from the street or by the neighbors, you haven't fully developed the possibilities of good living.

Once you establish privacy at the point you need it, you find many wonderful by-products begin to go into effect. You find your outdoor scene begins to belong to your indoors—and as a result your rooms seem bigger. You find yourself enlarging windows, which is good because the greater the flowing together of outdoors and indoors the bigger your house becomes—a good tip for anyone planning a new home. But it all begins with privacy.

Garden by James Rose

Hedge plus tree makes a sure stop again
those who would gaze, also cuts off view a
sound of passing traffic. You remain a frienc
neighbor but now enjoy privacy.

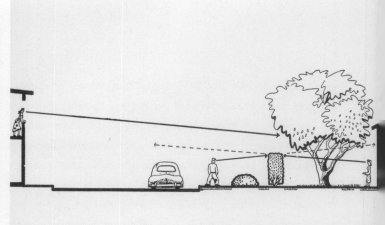

You can make a low fence do the work of
tall one that might make the neighbors tal
Trick is to build a raised bank around your lc
put the fence atop bank. You gain a raise
plant bed on your side (left photo). Bul
ground cover on your neighbor's side (acro
page) discourages over-the-fence talk.

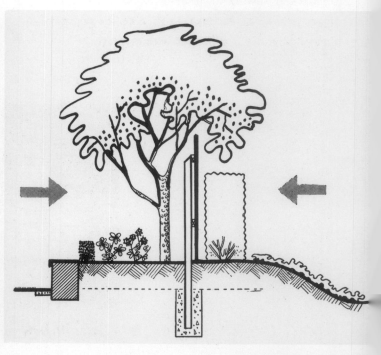

Garden by Thomas D. Church

Privacy doesn't mean isolation, and you needn't own a big lot. But you must cut off the view of those outside your yard. Then you can wear what you please, romp with the children and family pets, or spend the afternoon asleep in the hammock. This is as it should be. You wouldn't think of building a house that exposed you constantly to public view. Your back yard must be equally private to be usable.

Fences don't have to be completely solid if people will be passing in moving cars rather than walking. Weathered vertical boards make simple but handsome fence. Woven slats (above right) make highly decorative pattern.

Upper right garden by Vincent Merrill

Most of us can't afford to achieve privacy b
surrounding ourselves with empty acreage
But many of us overlook the front yard, thereb
wasting a third of the lot. Shown here are th
front yards of people who made the land wor
for them. They used an old device of the high
way builder and piled up a big mound of soil,
berm, planted heavily to extend protectio
from sight and sound still higher. Sometimes
hides the house from the street, as at the lef
where the mound hid the house completel
until the photographer stood on car to mak
the picture. But only a berm 10 feet high pro
tects you from the noise, fumes, and head
lights of truck traffic.

Gardens by Ralph W. Smith

Today's heavy traffic can't be ignored or talked out of existence. The abrasive effects of screeching brakes and honking horns, with grumbling gears and noxious fumes, are even more inhibiting to outdoor living than the watchful eyes of nosy neighbors. Unless you build barricades against these intrusions, you waste all that expensive front-yard land. But plant a heavy screen on a mound (above) or rely on a high berm (below), and you gain the privacy that makes it possible for all your land to work for you.

This is a city garden, added to an old house. Street trees were only asset: everything else has been added. Key, though, is the privacy assured by the new brick wall, which had to be kept low, so was erected 20 feet back from sidewalk to make it act like a high wall in stopping view from street.

ew garden was tucked between house and
g tree next to neighbor's house. Photograph
ustrates how passer-by can't see into gar-
en: table and chairs under umbrella are com-
etely out of sight, as would be people sitting
nywhere on the terrace.

rvice yard is hidden behind this rear wall and
te. Plants throughout garden were chosen
th discrimination, created handsome tex-
res summer and winter, reinforced by in-
resting shadow patterns.

Wall next to neighbor rises higher than along
street side but has been planted on both sides
with fine broad-leaved evergreens to give both
yards an especially attractive view.

Garden by Vincent Merrill

When the street is only 10 feet beyond your picture window, neither yard nor room is fully usable until you ensure your privacy.

Service yard is only 6 feet away from this doc but no one would think about it because th little garden between is so attractive.

Small garden below juts up against the neighbor's but seems spacious and colorful because of simplified planting (shrub hydrangea).

End panel of garden above opens (below) fc easy servicing of the small flower-show p garden. Vertical wood is bamboo poles.

Upper left garden by Paul Thiry
Lower left by Thomas D. Church

This "estate" occurs in a small, city back yard with numerous close neighbors on three sides. Transite fence belies its 6-feet height because of its color and the openness between walls and roof of the pool "house." Photographer was looking out from floor-to-ceiling glass wall of master bedroom. View (right) from off-street parking area shows "back" of fence.

Garden by Thomas D. Church

ront yard is given over to off-street parking
r six cars. Path acts as curb, ensures shrubs
gainst accidental bumps.

le-line wooden fence uses its own structure
create pattern and ever-changing shadows.

Curving concrete path leads from pool out to
side entrance at car port, gains apparent size
for yard because the curving lines and zigzag
catch and delight your eyes.

use at right ensures its own privacy by
pping around three sides of the terrace
urth side already heavily planted by
ture).

Lower right garden by Douglas Baylis

Well-kept hedges separate the neighbors in a friendly, effective way, for little cost.

When you have more than one terrace, each must be private from the next. Raising fence 12 inches off the ground lets breezes enter.

Hedges are hard to beat for garden ba grounds, waste space only if left untended.

Hardware cloth lets light into garden blocks view unless you stand directly in fr of it. This is fence anyone could build.

Lower right fence by Robert Deering

...ines lower visual height of privacy wall from ...reet side. Ground cover is strawberry.

...his picket fence deters trespassers but avoids ...forbidding appearance. Buy pickets ready-...ade, prime-coat, then attach while wet.

Private world outside your bedroom is one of life's great joys, requires little space. Hanging-vine treatment highly useful for blank walls.

Use stock materials with imagination: this is conventional corrugated asbestos board.

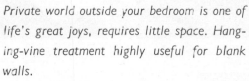

Upper right garden by George Hoy

When stone occurs naturally, you may want to build a rock wall for privacy. Here colorful rocks were piled between forms, and a rather dry concrete poured in to bind them. "Roof" of canvas cuts out heat and glare of desert sky.

Wide baffles provide adequate eye screen from all but the one direction photographer used to show construction of this privacy screen. Panels contain frosted glass.

Upper garden by Frank Lloyd Wright
Lower by Berkeley Women's City Club

ortable privacy screen—from eyes and wind
—rolls easily on large casters. Also useful
hen late afternoon sun annoys you.

Lacy fence is made of standard structural tile
that cost about 16¢ each. Pattern is so bold that
it distracts eyes from seeing beyond. Openness
allow breezes to pass freely.

Portable screen by Thomas Windemere
Tile wall by Fehr & Granger

Upper garden by Robert Royston
Lower left by Kathryn I. Stedman

our privacy fences can be works of art.
anslucent fence above contains jewel-
lored plaques of modern stained glass by
rence Swift, but skillful use of light and
adow also shows other possibilities in
eating a work-of-art fence.

Other four examples use conventional
ilding materials, including the Fiberglas-
lyester plastic panel (right), in new ways.
ture uses of these products depend only
on the ingenuity of the fence designers.
any products are so lightweight they are
stly easier to handle than any previous fence
aterial, so require much less bulky supports,
o less brawn for erection.

Fence upper right is rough-sawed boards
ed in louver effects. Ask the local lumberyard
cut all the pieces to size: you merely nail
em into position to build the fence.

Upper right garden by John Funk
Lower right by James Cowan

Pre-school children like to climb—in, over, an
through things. Older children quickly tire
climbing, unless it is to a tree house. All pla
equipment can be good art, as evidence
by the tree-trunk jungle or this tree hous
Children naturally love beauty: expose the
to it.

Chapter 13

Boys want a pirate ship: a simple affair of old boards, bright paint, and a bedsheet sail will do. But girls want a quiet place where they can talk to fairies, stable imaginary horses, or just dream. Give them such a place and they'll find something new to do each day.

The garden is for children, too

Children are happiest when they are doing something. They like to run, jump, swing, slide, climb, balance, hang, or shout. They tire quickly, though, so filling the yard with "official" play equipment provides no guarantee that they will be happy. You have to stimulate self-activity. Give them things their imagination can work on—sand and water and things easy to move, like boxes, boards, barrels, ladders, and saw-horses. Such objects are suggestive, easily adapted to any imaginary situation by any age. They make the back yard a wonderful land of make-believe. Children then never run out of "something new to do" if you provide:

1. Paved trike run.
2. Something to climb on, preferably trees.
3. Lawn space for tumbling and wrestling.
4. A place to dig.
5. Water to play in—and a place for mud pies.
6. Convenient toilet and hand-washing facilities.
7. Sturdy seating that doesn't have to be pampered or rushed indoors when rain threatens.
8. Eating facilities, preferably with barbecue.
9. Covered, rainy-day play space.
10. Outdoor dance floor.
11. Sturdy plants that can survive accidents.
12. Raised plant beds to keep plants out of the way.
13. Fences rather than hedges.
14. Scuff-proof paths.
15. Easy, quick storage for play gear.
16. Complete isolation from automobiles.
17. Adequate climate control—choice of sun or shade, ample breezes, protection from insects and dust.

Children "lost" in the world of make-believe forget the ABC rules of safety, so fence in the play yard so there can be no auto accidents. Keep bike runs free of blind corners.

Play yards needn't look messy, but you can't expect children to keep things tidied up, so install a strong ground pattern that keeps the eyes from noticing scattered toys. Outdoor blackboard makes popular addition to yard.

Lower playground by George Kruegal

Mother should be able to keep the entire play yard in view without leaving her household activities. Seat wall doubles as guard against wheeled toys bumping into flowers.

Space is used most efficiently when various play activities are kept separate, makes house-keeping easier, too. Fence may be simple barrier, or may double as window, as here.

Playgrounds by Imlay & Scott

The garden is for children, too

Ideal playground for young children, a shaded tanbark-covered area confined within the bold lines of its seat wall.

Sometimes the play yard can be a separate but visual part of the over-all garden. This one has a complete storage wall for toys.

When play space is visually part of the main garden, play equipment must be sited to look good from the terrace—or be off to one side and behind shrubs, as here.

Upper garden by Kathryn I. Stedman
Center by Osmundson & Staley
Lower by Douglas Baylis

No play surface is better than a good lawn, but no grass can survive daily pounding. If your play area is so small that it gets no rest, then you must pave. Brick on sand is fine for games that require non-skid footing, tanbark better for rough-and-tumble.

Here yard was big enough so that children could have separate play area adjacent to their own wing of the house. Strong pattern of bike run makes interesting ground lines.

Night-lighting the play area greatly enhances its value, especially to teen-agers and for games whole family can play, like badminton.

Upper garden by Douglas Baylis
Center & lower gardens by Thomas D. Church

Children grow up so fast that today's needs are past as soon as tomorrow. This means that expensive solutions should have convertibility to be realistic. The sand "box" gets heavy traffic only until school starts, then becomes "baby stuff." But while it is in use the child needs supervision, so locate it near the house. Later sandbox can become a big flower garden, a panel of lawn grass, or a mosaic of dwarf plants.

The trike run easily shifts into a roller rink, and then still later into a dance floor, all without disrupting the basic garden design.

A play yard without a swing is unthinkable. Make it strong, and low at first, easily adjusted as young legs stretch and need room.

Children will stay in what you hopefully call "play space" only if it is the place they enjoy most in the whole yard.

Garden by Thomas D. Church

283

The garden is for children, too

Play shouldn't disturb the neighbors by its noises, dust, or looks. This neat, sensible solution serves a family of six young children. Later the play yard will become a swimming pool.

Sandbox for visiting grandchildren will soon be turned into a colorful flower bed for terrace

Upper garden by Thomas D. Church
Lower garden by Edward Huntsman-Trout

This house takes advantage of its site by creating an upper terrace for the adults, a lower for the children, directly off playroom. Lower view illustrates ease of visual supervision of lower terrace.

Garden by Bryan J. Lynch

...een-agers need a place for entertaining ...oups of friends—and to take the wear off the ...ouse, nothing is better than a good outdoor ...ing room like this. It provides kitchen facili... ...es, storage of extra furniture, plus its own ...wder room.

Older teen-agers may want a house for their hobbies. A house like this, here arranged for woodworking, could be the center of any collection activity, a dress-designing studio, or a place to make a bow, boat, or new styling for a teen-ager's jalopy.

Only a person who has operated and maintained the tools of a craft really knows the pleasure of extending your power of control over the world around you. If you drive a car, you have that pleasure—provided that you feel secure in your ability to make minor adjustments and repairs without limping into a garage every time you flood the carburetor. It is the kind of pleasure you want your children to experience.

Providing a house for a craft, whether weaving or printing, is today's way of extending play facilities beyond the traditional play years—and of ensuring more interesting lives.

Left garden by Hannah Champlin
Craft house by Harwell H. Harris

When the house is small, the garden must double as living and play space, stand up to the wear and tear of continuous use. You can use only plants that stay presentable, that need no fussy care, that please you by their daily presence in your life. Obviously your yard won't resemble the traditional garden—or the usual play yard. Rather, it will look like a comfortable big living room that gets much love and use. This is what the owners of the garden on these two pages discovered.

Raised plant beds get the flowers out of the way of lawn games, display them nearer to eye level, make garden keeping easier. Fence ensures wind protection, reflects sunlight and heat. Concrete mowing strip eliminates need for hand trimming lawn.

Dwarf fruit trees espaliered against south-facing fence fruit remarkably well, require little space, cast highly decorative shadows. Ground cover below tree is variegated ivy.

Important, difficult spots can be decorated with a tree or a few bold plants able to fend for themselves—far left, a rice-paper plant. Use only one kind of plant: mixing always increases upkeep.

Garden by Thomas D. Church

Collecting stones like these for an attractiv mulch around trees and in odd-angle corner makes a good first step in introducing your children to the wonderful world of gardenin

Given only 25 by 72 feet, this owner managed to get play space for young children, a clothes-drying yard, a flower garden, a stylish dining terrace and a panel of lawn grass—plus a feeling of unconfined outdoor living. Secret lies in the planning that eliminated need to devote any area exclusively to one function.

Raised beds of some easy-to-grow plant make interesting companions for play yards, may catch a child's attention and make him wish to try his hand at growing something. Children respond to what they see in their daily lives. Don't overlook the chance to expose them to the best while they play.

Upper garden by Douglas Baylis
Lower by Imlay & Scott

The garden is for children, too

In an area that was for years little more than a trash heap, new owners saw a chance to produce a useful play yard for their children, had the whole job done for $400, which included all the labor too.

View toward side neighbor was pleasant, s open-grid fence merely marks boundary with out interrupting view. Panels hide his laundr yard, serve also as blackboards for owner children. Plantings emphasize texture.

Garden by Larry Halprin

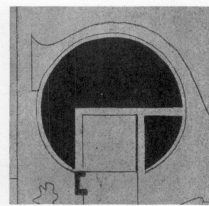

vimming pools are rapidly becoming common
play yards. They pose serious design prob-
ms because they are so big. The three ready-
ade pools—rectangular, oval, and "classic"
—put drastic limitations on what you can do.
hey look best in big gardens with long sweeps
lawn to set them off—and definitely out of
ace on most small lots.

Custom-designed pools look better and
e the available space more efficiently. You
rive at the correct shape by manipulating
e terraces, paths, and plantings any way you
e, then shaping the pool to fit the space that
mains. You do not start out with some
stract art form for the pool.

The six swimming pools, right and below,
olved as the logical answers to design prob-
ms created by the needs of the owners and
eir sites. They are unusual shapes, but per-
ctly good ones aesthetically, emphasizing
at you shouldn't be afraid to let your pool

take any shape it must take to utilize the space
best.

Pools like these may cost 15 to 30 per cent
more than stock shapes, but the extra costs
entailed in trying to alter the rest of the yard
to make a stock pool fit would have eaten up
much more than this. Even steel pools can be
custom-designed for such a low premium that
you shouldn't accept the handicap involved in
forcing your garden and your living to fit some
preconceived shape of pool.

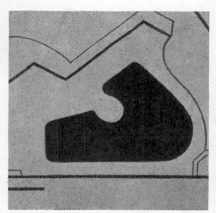

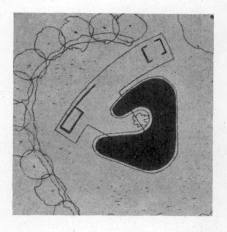

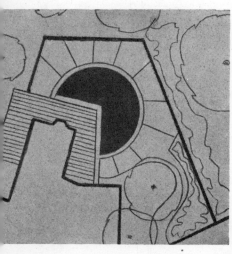

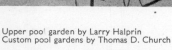
Upper pool garden by Larry Halprin
Custom pool gardens by Thomas D. Church

If sunshine reaches the area for 6 hours
day, you can grow most anything. When le
than this, shift to shade gardening.

Garden by Douglas Baylis

Chapter 14

Solving the shade problem

Shade poses two problems. The first, insufficient light for good plant health, gets the most attention. Actually it merits the lesser importance. Many plants grow rather well without receiving direct sunshine. Other plants, nominally sun plants, look better when protected from burning sun, especially in their pale pastel varieties.

Problem number two, inability to compete for food and water, often goes unnoticed. Old trees, for example, complete with huge root systems, rob the soil. Norway maples offer the most common example. Grass and flowers rarely succeed under Norway maples because the greedy roots fill the soil right to the surface. It's not the shade, *per se*, that causes this "shade problem."

There is no practical *planting* solution to the Norway maple problem, other than a ground cover of ivy, myrtle, or pachysandra. Other kinds of trees allow you to garden beneath them if you supply extra food and water regularly. You must supply enough of both so that the tree gets its fill, with a surplus available to your other plants. Then, to be sure that the shade doesn't become too dense from the well-fed growth, you should thin the tree regularly and gradually "lift" its lower-branch height to let light reach your garden below.

Cool, quiet retreat from hot sun shows how few other plants are needed to make a garden when dancing shadows are used importantly in the over-all designing.

295

Solving the shade problem

Shade gardens necessarily must let green pre-
dominate. But add striking shadows and other
colors aren't missed. Curving line makes area
appear much bigger than its 50-foot size.

You can have a panel of green lawn grass sun
or shade, easy way to tie together your garden
composition when trees make pools of shade
too heavy for flowers.

Put your terrace in the shade, more comfortable for you, more practical for the plants
which now get moved out into sunny areas.
Terrace here "flows" out, making whole yard
seem much bigger.

Thick, handsome hedges are big helpers when
you are creating gardens in shade.

Use pots of such shade plants as these caladiums (color photograph on page 211) or tuberous begonias to brighten the heavy shadows. Paving here is brick laid on sand, allowing rain to soak down to tree roots.

Patio within a house gets sun just a few hours a day because of shade from house itself but can be gardened successfully, as here. Grow plants in pots, move them in when ready to make their best blossoms or leaf display. Confine lawn to center, the sunniest part of such a patio.

This narrow strip between house and lot line is so fully planted that visitors entering garden through it aren't aware that this is major "flower garden" of whole yard.

Gardens by Marie & Arthur Berger

Solving the shade problem

This lawn receives direct sunlight only at midday because of the way the trees have been placed.

Plant trees first. You must have an abundance of shade trees, all well established before any garden can stay fresh and green in a 100° region. You can move in big trees for quick shade if you are willing to pay the initial cost and upkeep. Gardens planted in one season, though, suffer from drouth and won't look very fresh the first few years.

...esign the garden so that it is developed ...tensively. Make every square foot contribute ...o the look of greenness. Do this by partition-...ng garden into "use" areas, each giving depth ...f focus to the next, making the garden seem ...o go on and on "with more greenness just ...round the corner."

This central Texas garden survives weeks of weather 100° to 105° because it is a shade garden. No direct sunlight penetrates the dense canopy of tree shade in any spot for more than an hour a day.

Shade is indispensable in 100° weather, as much for garden plants as for man. No amount of watering can make up for a lack of shade. Roots just can't absorb water as fast as the heat evaporates it from the leaves. They wilt. Then the plants look tired and droopy in the landscape.

More than this, brilliant sunlight on a 100° day is so bright that it solarizes the leaves of most plants, bringing the normal food-making machinery of the leaves to a halt. In effect the plant starves, adding to its moisture-shortage troubles.

How, then, do shade trees survive? Their sheer mass stands them in good stead. The upper leaves do wilt and do solarize. But the shaded leaves below are protected, so function normally. And of course the roots of big trees go deep into the soil, drawing water up from a vast territory which smaller plants can't reach. Obviously young trees must be watered and fed generously to help compensate for their smaller root spread and their inability to provide self-shade. Under severe conditions it may be wise to protect them, at least for the first year or two, by erecting an overhead screen or trellis.

Fifteen years ago this garden was a flat, treeless city lot. The owners decided to plant young trees at once but to delay garden build-ing until the trees were established. Big trees could have been moved in, of course. But they would have suffered severely for a number of years. It is axiomatic that any new garden will suffer terribly. Don't expect a garden to look lush and green until it is both shaded and established. Patience is important in garden building in hot climates.

Seven years ago the shade was adequate to start the garden shown here. Today it is a model of the stylish garden possible in a 100° region.

Garden by Marie & Arthur Berger

This planting hides the service yard from view of visitors. To maintain luxuriant growth like this, keep gardens small enough for you to be able to give good care even in the hottest weather when you won't want to devote much time to gardening. Many well-intentioned people make a big mistake here.

Hot-climate gardening calls for shade overhead and no large expanses of direct sunlight. If you want more garden than you have shade, plant trees now in the unshaded areas but wait until the new trees grow up before incorporating these areas into your garden.

Welcome shade everywhere helps banish the glare that makes even healthy plants look hot and tired. Hot-climate garden must be basically a green garden, but you can tuck in flowers by the front door and in other shade-protected places.

Choose mainly from the drouth-resistant and heat-tolerant plants, especially those native to your region. Ask your local landscape nurseryman about these. The choice of species is quite extensive, although many nurserymen don't bother with these plants because so many people hate to pay nursery prices for plants that can be seen growing wild in the area.

Plants fighting a tough climate need extra food as well as water. Well-fed plants can stretch a limited moisture supply surprisingly far. This is the narrow strip between the house and the lot next door, owned by the same family. Decision to ignore chance to use vacant lot was wise. Don't exceed your time budget in any gardening. It's fatal to do so when growing conditions are bad

Spring gardens provide one reliable answer to the shade problem. At no other time of year are the shadows as interesting. The sunlight now falls in long, slanting rays. Tree leaves remain too small to cut off much light, and so thin that sunlight readily shines through them to give a color like lush new grass. The spring bulbs make spectacular bids for attention. They look their best with sun in their faces, but thrive even in complete shade if started fresh from new bulbs each year. Probably no other flower is as sure to please you when shade is deep.

Garden by Rose Greeley

Upper pool by Ernest Wertheim

Garden pools are such wonderful shadow catchers that we often fail to remember them when building a shade garden. Yet pools in the shade provide delightful additions, bringing sound and motion to replace the reliance upon flower color.

Stylish pools are surprisingly simple to build. These six would fit either modern or traditional gardens, illustrate that pool doesn't have to be big to be effective. Saucer across page is only 16 inches deep. Small birdbath far lower left is simply a stone hollowed naturally. Concrete pool below is only 8 inches deep.

Small, ivy-ringed pool above could be made by a beginning amateur in metalworking. Ivy collar hides any rough edges. Needle jet is merely copper tube squeezed shut, then pinholed at the top. Sound of this small amount of falling water adds pleasantly to garden. Excess water evaporates or runs over into always-thirsty ivy.

Steel bowls of various sizes and shapes can be bought ready-made, or a local welding shop can make any you sketch to fit your needs. Or you may find what you want among modern barbecue bowls. Big bowl in lower right photo was cut from an old boiler, a job for the junk yard's acetylene torch.

Upper garden by George Siebenthaler
Lower left by Osmundson & Staley
Lower right by Larry Halprin

Garden by John Yeon

Right: The form that water takes in the garden often is more important than its reflections.

Size of pool determines size of plants and kinds of foliage textures to use. The pools below and across page are especially beautiful because their designers gave detailed attention to scale in choosing plants. Many people err here, overcrowding the pool with huge water-lilies. Really small pools look best when all plants grow outside the pool rather than in it.

Waterfalls, must be in scale with the size of the pool. Water here comes from a small recirculating pump, seems completely natural.

Lower garden by Clarence Prentice

Too often a garden pool occurs as an afterthought stuck in an out-of-the-way corner. It deserves to be the very heart of a garden, especially the shade garden. Water appeals as attractively to the eye and imagination as an equal area of concentrated bloom.

But you don't have to rely on water alone for pool interest. Put your pool in a planted flagstone setting. Then you can have flowers in the spring from bulbs, flowers in the summer from pot plants moved into place when in bloom. Some can be set down into the soil. Others can sit in their pots as welcome, colorful visitors while at their flower-show best.

The photographs here show how decorative a combination pool and rock garden can be. It is built in the center of a circle of lawn surrounded on all sides by rapidly growing shade trees that will soon shut off all but an hour or so of sun each day. But, unlike many rock gardens and pools, this one offers a touch of formality. It provides a change of levels, always interesting to the eyes, plus a change of materials for an area that otherwise would be flat and unoriginal.

lat, thick field stones make ideal shallow teps. They can be laid dry (without mortar), ccommodating low rock plants in the crannies. f you use flagstones instead, better add a concrete footing in frost area. Scoop out the joints nd sprinkle mortar with soil while wet to tone own the whiteness.

Garden by Thomas D. Church

Water needn't be deep to reflect the changin
moods of a garden. Leaves and branche
passing clouds, changing shadows, all 'ea
their momentary imprints.

Restrict your planting to a few kinds of plant
boldly displayed for a stylish result. Pair
bottom of a shallow pool deep black to make
better reflector.

Upper garden by Robert Mosher

Tiny pool only two inches deep, set on the edge of the lawn and fringed by low plants, catches reflections of sky and trees as well as larger pool. You can move it easily to enjoy new settings.

Deep water offers one great advantage in garden planning. It takes on the changing colors of the sky overhead. Shrubs are spring-blooming, make their big growth of the year before the shade trees cut off much of the direct sunshine.

Coolness for a terrace, this jet of water splashing into a little pool adds enough interest so that near absence of flowers isn't noticed. Pool is only six inches deep.

Gardens by Allen Dalsime

Garden by Thomas D. Church

This was a gully too steep to be of any use to the family. Raised deck juts out into space, with trees coming up to it from lower level. Grass panel and hedge border are on regraded bit of land, held up on either side by retaining walls.

Deck garden enables owners to enjoy comfort and privacy outdoors. Garden and deck measure only 28 by 48 feet, seem far bigger because design was kept so simple. There are close neighbors behind the bushy trees.

Garden slopes and hill sites

Many people forgo outdoor living because the yard offers no place level enough for a terrace. The problem is not new but has become acute in many areas because all the level house lots have already been built upon. As a result, much thought has been given to find ways to convert unwanted, "bad" land into useful homesites. Today many landscape architects rate the problem site as the most attractive buy for people planning to build. These designers also rate as good buys many of the houses built in recent years on hillside lots without provision for outdoor living.

This reversal of values owes much to the development of engineering interest in deck building. Spanning sizable areas is no longer a trial-and-error process but is a science practiced by trained landscape contractors who know they can cantilever great decks out into a treetop garden without trouble.

Decks free you from the need to build heavy retaining walls, haul in prodigious amounts of fill, or get involved in extensive, expensive regrading. Decks usually can start with what the site offers, get their support from simple footing and posts. Whatever plant growth exists on the land usually can be saved, maybe even to poke up through the deck floor. You suffer none of the raw newness of regraded land, no aggravated erosion while waiting for a new ground-saving plant cover to grow.

Letting a deck solve your site problem may result in three enormous gains in distinction for your garden and the outdoor living it makes possible. You may gain a superb view, one that shoots out to the horizon, missing the tops of nearby houses, making your lot seem huge, with you "owning" the view as far as you can see.

Or you may gain another kind of privacy, that of intimate shelter, surrounded by a network of trees left to grow up around the deck, as in the upper view across page.

Certainly the floor of your deck can be distinctive in style, as the variations on the next pages illustrate. This pattern can fulfill much of the need for interest from flowers, especially when pots and tubs of interesting plants are to be grown on the new deck. The very real roomlike quality of a deck with railing makes the few plants as important in decorating as are plants in indoor rooms.

Decks are not inexpensive. Flooring and floor joists cost $2 to $3 a square foot. Footings and post supports vary so widely in cost that figures depend heavily upon the site. But suppose you do spend $4 to $6 for each square foot of complete deck, maybe even $7 to $8 in "impossible" situations. For this you have bought superb living space, probably the most useful in your house, often the most dramatic.

Millions of fine old houses were built before America discovered the joy of modern indoor-outdoor living. Most of these houses sit up on high foundations. Getting in or out involves climbing three or four steps, which puts a psychological barrier between you and your garden.

It is easy to add a modern terrace to such a house without costly regrading. The solution is to build a deck at the same level with the floor indoors. Then you get an unbroken relationship between indoors and out, which improves the usability of both. There is a size and style of deck for every kind of house and budget.

Don't worry about spoiling the looks of a good old house by adding a good modern terrace or deck. It can make your old house look better sited by tying it down to the ground visually. Your house will appear to rest more solidly on its new structural platform, eliminating the "stuck-up" look that so clearly dates many old houses.

The deck can be completely self-supporting, entirely independent of the house and exerting no pressure on the foundation wall. Natural drainage patterns in the soil remain unchanged, and air circulates freely under a deck. This is important if tree roots occur in the area. Major regrading often smothers and kills trees.

The deck that works like a terrace is sure to bring a major change in the way the family lives because it makes outdoor living more readily available. Consider adding a deck before dismissing the modernization of an otherwise fine old house.

Gardens by Thomas D. Church

Beach-front houses often are left without gar
dens because shifting sands so readily wipe ou
the gardener's effort. Add a sturdy terrac
deck like this instead.

When the ground falls away abruptly, a deck
is worth almost any cost. This one cantilevers
into space as a monolithic concrete slab sup
ported part way by fill. Deck was included
when house was built. If added later, pier
supported deck would have been more eco
nomical.

Upper garden by Thomas D. Church
Lower by Stanley Underhill

Decks aren't limited to any specific height. This living-room terrace juts out a full story above ground, with cantilever support rather than visible posts—good idea for high decks.

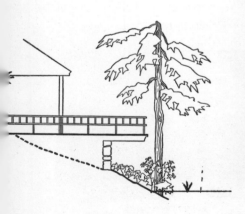

Uphill view of deck shown on opposite page illustrates how little planting is needed for a lush, gardened look to a deck that puts you up into the branches of the trees.

Sometimes you should dig down, make you[r] terrace at the low level of the slope.

Small wall like this saves enormous amounts o[f] fill, permits grade to change pleasantly in tw[o] directions at once.

Privacy is assured by wall **(below)** much higher than permitted by local zoning rules if not needed as retaining wall.

Photographer stood on a ladder on the side-walk, looking down into garden across page.

Add steps and a grade change becomes visually important, an asset in garden design.

Below: Turn a wall back on itself rather than allow it to peter away. Method also anchors the wall and holds bank firmly.

Right: When construction dictates that house must be more than one step above the grade, consider the raised terrace, extending out at floor level or just a low step below.

Left: Raised area is both path and terrace partially roofed by the overhang of house.

Left: Retaining walls here make possible a sizable addition to the living space, protect the tree roots, allow necessary regrading for quick runoff of rain.

Right: Terrace within the "U" of this house does occur at lower level but broad top platform and wide steps make transition pleasant both to view and to use.

Garden by James M. Fitch

Garden by John L. King

This terrace sits above the garden with no steps between house and terrace, exposes people to any welcome, stray summer breezes (central Texas).

Tree was moved in after new grade was established, made eye-catching from every view. Brickwork here is exceptionally fine.

Walls are corbeled, making it more comfortable to sit upon (place for your feet), more dramatic in shadow line.

Garden by Marie & Arthur Berger,
Installed by Houston B. Bliss

Once this was the "back door" and the way
the land fell away from the house was unimportant. But that was when nice people were
chauffeured to an elegant front door and only
the car and driver ever saw the rear view.
Now, with just about everyone driving, the
motor court is the front door.

A covered entrance was ruled out here because it would have darkened the house too
much. Solution was an overhead trellis that
provides a sense of protection, plus luxurious
spaciousness rivaling that of approaches to

Old World castles. All the drop in grade no
comes at the entrance steps, handsomely ar
importantly scaled.

Exciting shadow play is by-product of good design by a man who knows wood—no mere crisscross of ordinary 2 by 4's but delicately detailed 2 by 8's for the strong black lines. Beam thins as it reaches past last support, ends in a cut-back angle that further stresses lightness. Result is an airy screen like drifting clouds overhead instead of a weight intent upon crushing down upon you.

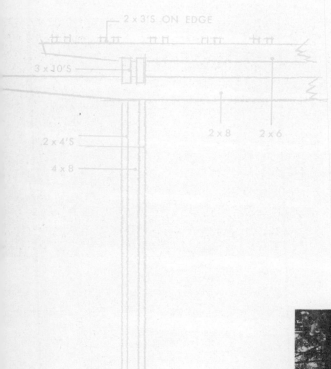

2 x 3'S ON EDGE

3 x 10'S

2 x 4'S

4 x 8

2 x 8   2 x 6

The clump of old redwoods (below and across page) now makes a spectacular view as you stand in new "front" door and look back toward entrance from motor court. Fortunately they block off both south and west sun heat. Big paved patio thus offers innumerable choices of where to sit, and all for little more cost than for a conventional wide front path.

Garden by Thomas D. Church

Let a flight of handsome steps be the garden for an entrance too steep to plant. Cheek wall at left of steps serves as retaining wall, also contributes aesthetically with its bold, curved line and fine texture.

Building blocks, filled with good garden soil and planted, make a quick, attractive way to hold a bank that threatens to wash away. Common mistake is to attempt to put such an area into lawn grass, which can't hope to do well under such difficult growing conditions.

Even slopes twice this steep can be held in place with a heavy shrub planting. But use well-rooted plants. Don't skimp and buy "bargains," as many find themselves tempted to do by the need for using large numbers of plants at one time. Good idea, too, to inter-plant with a ground cover to delay further erosion-producing runoff of rains.

Wrap a strong, curving line from one level to the next and you can wipe out the change as far as the quick look is concerned. Allowing plants on lower level to grow a bit taller also helps with this illusion.

Garden across page by Thomas D. Church

Steepness of slope isn't always the critical factor. In the garden sketched below as it existed, the slope was insignificant. The real problem was the lack of connection between the first floor and the back yard, complicated by the digging out of soil to make possible an exit from the basement to the trash-storing area.

Thousands of older houses suffer this same way. They were built when it was fashionable to expose the basement fully on the street side, partially bury it in the slope of the back

yard. Opening such a house "for garden living" is much more than adding a pair of french doors and a flight of steps.

Solution here uses a deck at floor level, extending out over the lower half of the yard. Now whole area behind the house works for the family, glamorous living on the upper level, more workable service, and storage space below deck where digging out made root space for a new shade tree.

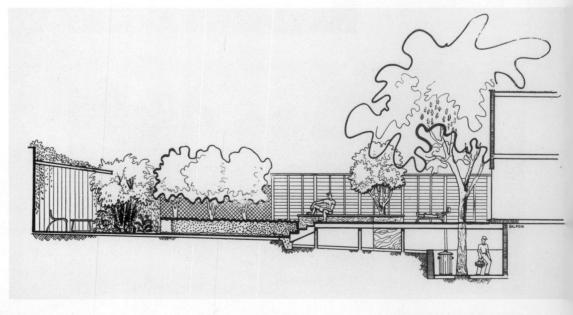

Garden shelter by Thomas D. Church

Gently sloping lawns like this often are left untouched. Here imaginative handling created a sense of heightened slope that places the house atop a sizable hill. Planting behind the stepped-back stone wall prevents your eyes from discovering whether or not steepness of slopes requires such a high wall to hold the slope.

Garden by John Grant

329

This garden is twenty-four hours old, created for the International Flower Show in New York but later duplicated outdoors a dozen times.

Landscapes without waiting

For years gardens were planted with the idea that they would look skimpy for the first ten or fifteen years. "After all, you are planting for future generations," used to be the idea. But now with the typical family in a house only five years, a new interest has developed in gardens to enjoy right now.

Planting a "full-grown" garden probably costs less than you think. True, big plants cost more than baby plants. But when the garden is designed and planted with choice, mature plants, you need few plants. Prices of mature plants naturally vary greatly because these are one-of-a-kind art treasures. But in general the prices remain surprisingly reasonable, because there really isn't much of a market for them. Few people have discovered what they can do for a garden. Others *assume* the cost is too high. Before you order a dozen or two of any shrub, mentally calculate the visual effect of just one really great specimen of the shrub you plan to buy.

Once you have the few key plants, the rest can be the low-cost, baby sizes. These plants will be as inconspicuous in the over-all design as is a single grass plant in your new lawn.

Ideally, you will put the planning project in charge of a talented landscape architect and the planting under the direction of an experienced landscape nurseryman (quite different from an ordinary nurseryman or a door-to-door bush peddler).

Homeowners are often puzzled by the wide variety of prices quoted for the same landscape work. A spread of 100 per cent often occurs. The high bidder probably plans to supply big, bushy plants, the low bidder light, stringy plants just getting under the grade limit for height. Low bidders usually include a lump sum for planting. High bidders usually itemize exactly what they plan to do—size of holes, amounts of peat and loam to be furnished, amount and brand of plant food and grass seed, plus a specific labor charge.

Labor for planting varies drastically. A small evergreen 2 feet high has a 12-inch ball of soil, will fit in a 12-inch hole. This requires the removal of only $\frac{1}{2}$ cubic foot of soil. But the 2-foot plant should have a hole 30 by 18 inches—nearly $7\frac{1}{2}$ cubic feet of soil to be removed, or 14 times the work. And maybe the soil is so poor that it should be wheelbarrowed away and new soil brought in.

The most foolish economy in landscaping is cheap planting methods. It often is fatal when you are buying big, mature plants for quick effects. It is more important to check the reputation of your landscape nurseryman than his prices. You are buying service, not a competitive product.

Garden by Allen Dalsimer

Landscapes without waiting

How long will a garden-for-now last? Obviously all plants grow, so even though your new garden looks full-grown from its first day, the plants will continue to increase in size. The increase is negligible in the key plants, the big plants bought in mature size. The other plants, the inconspicuous background greens and grays, may need some annual pruning, but they should last ten years before getting noticeably out of scale.

Gardens need a revamping every ten years. Natural hazards of wind and ice, new pests, and major changes in climate because of new buildings nearby or natural tree growth in adjacent gardens make this necessary.

Plants shouldn't be your first thought in garden building. Rather, think first and invest first in the construction part of your garden—grading, paving, walls, and fences. You see here the start of work for the motor court of the garden across page.

This garden is six months old. Even the trees were moved in. Today the skilled landscape nurseryman can move a plant of almost any size with reasonable assurance. Naturally most of the big plants he offers are one-of-a-kind, true crt pieces in horticulture. This enables you to decorate outdoors as you do indoors—with a few choice pieces.

Garden by Webel & Innocenti

Another view of garden shown on page 330. Wall adds interest of two-level gardening to what was a perfectly flat piece of ground.

Left below: Handsome rock work plus a few plants, but it looks as though this garden had been growing happily here for years.

Right below: Detail step-back on the low wall makes it more inviting to sit on, adds eye-catching shadow lines at no cost.

Garden by Allen Dalsimer

Except for the wisteria vines whole garden has just been added. Plants are few but choice. Shrub with bold trunk outline against brick wall is Pieris, more commonly seen as a tight, globular shrub. Judicious pruning of an old, overgrown plant gave it new form.

This was view before porch gave way to a room and stylish garden and terrace were added.

Garden by Edwin T. Wyatt

Owners replaced one wall of house with glass, created from a few superb plants a garden worthy of being part of daily living.

Most interesting plants are kept close to the glass for enjoying even on winter days when people don't want to walk in garden.

Garden was installed in completed form, ready to use and enjoy for less than $1000 in New York's Westchester County.

Garden by Rosedale Landscape Nursery

Treasure of the garden is this tiny pool and its garden of diminutive evergreens, selected individually for their beauty.

Below: San Francisco terrace garden, permanent structure plus a few sturdy plants. Garden was complete on day planted.

Garden by Osmundson & Staley

Landscapes without waiting

Site for this Pace-Setter House was chosen for its trees. All other planting occurred in the ten days before "after" photographs were made. Plants were chosen for their individual contributions to the over-all beauty. There are no unimportant plants used "to hide the foundation." Result is a series of interesting garden views rather than the old-fashioned, costly-to-maintain mustache of green "foundation planting."

Screen of broad-leaved evergreens makes use of front yard for off-street parking more acceptable to an ultra-conservative area. Boundary lines for the black-top paving curve gracefully, have no hard corners as in commercial parking lots. Result is handsome, useful space from that third of the house lot so often unused by its owners.

Individually these evergreens would be classified as non-salable by the usual roadside nursery, but collectively and in the hands of a sensitive designer they create a distinctive little garden. Now the leggy, irregular growth that made them "unsalable" contributes importantly. Visit a landscape nurseryman to find plants like these.

Baffled entrance to service yard has only two plants, both broad-leaved evergreens. One at right has been espaliered.

House was slipped under and between the trees, looked like this a few weeks before plantsman created view across page.

Winter view of espaliered pear tree seen in autumn across page. They are an important art form, give quick "finish" to garden.

Garden by Thomas D. Church

Today's kitchen garden stays neat all season

Confine kitchen garden between brick-paved paths and, whether freshly planted, luxuriantly full in midseason as here, or almost harvested, garden remains neat, one that people remember with pleasure.

Permanent color and pattern from pavings call for much planning, often can be executed rapidly, making new garden inviting from its earliest days. Using divider boards helps keep paving units in uniform rows, adds pattern of its own.

This garden is 18 hours old, created for the California Spring Garden Show. Paving is crushed brick, held in by redwood 2 by 4's stained black. When weather turns warm and pansies cease blooming, replace, perhaps, with petunias, zinnias, or marigolds for summer bloom, followed by chrysanthemums for fall color. Pool shown in color, page 304.

When garden can't be planted until late fa
make sizable groupings of spring bulbs. Th
garden was planted previous December (Co
necticut).

Petal sunshade of canvas laced into met
frame makes an eye-catcher people remembe
important item for too new gardens.

Pave a little area, confine it with a low brick
wall, and corner of garden stands ready to
work for you as pleasant living space.

Don't compete with handsome architecture.
Let it be the garden. Confine your planting to a
few plants, here the tracery of delicate vines.

Instead of rushing into buying trees and shrubs,
live with your new house until you know what
you need in the way of a garden. Wait to discover what parts of your yard will be most
livable at different times of year. Meantime,
get a good lawn started and rely on a few
flowering shrubs for first-year color.

Shadow-box design of screening fence provides
a foil for a pot garden that appears "complete"
as soon as installed on the shelves.

Upper fence by Frank Lloyd Wright

*Wild flowers, given loving care and good grow-
ing conditions, respond with a promising lushness few ''garden flowers'' can equal. Protect
the native flora from being trampled underfoot
during house building, or bring in big slabs of
the native field sod from where wild flowers
grow on your lot. Your garden can look complete the first year, grow in beauty with the
passing years as the wild flowers reseed and
spread.*

This dooryard planting keeps its good looks all year, bursts into handsome bloom several times a year because of its different plants.

This house needs no shrubs. Its sycamore maples and field of wild flowers are the garden. Consider long before starting to plant shrubs about a newly acquired old house. Time may have provided a better garden than what at first thought seems right for improving the new possession.

This garden house offers modern efficiency,
yet it looks very much at home as an extension
of the Victorian house because the best design
lines of the house are used again outdoors to
merge the old and the new.

Chapter 17

Remodeling the old garden

Bringing an old garden up to date involves changes more fundamental than those of "style" or period. It involves the reason for having a garden. Today we have a garden because we want to be outdoors as much as possible, even when we entertain. We expect the garden to give us privacy, physical comfort, and restful quietness in a noisy machine age. We insist that it pamper us. This is all very foreign to the thinking that prevailed when many fine old houses were built. But it does not force us to forgo outdoor living just because the house is of another era.

Gardens by Thomas D. Church

This 45-year-old garden was left untouched, the house remodeled, and a new terrace garden added—for terrace living (see opposite page).

Millions of houses in America have back yards that are pleasant—in a way. They are "landscaped" in a style popular some years ago—something to look at, more work than pleasure. It is hard to reach the garden from the living room. There's no place to put furniture, and no privacy for entertaining friends. There's no out-of-sight place to dry swim suits, store firewood, or keep the dog.

Marrying the old and the new poses no insurmountable difficulties. You start by assessing what exists. Decide what is worth saving, looking first at the trees. Huge old trees may have just about exhausted their will to live. Fussing with them is expensive. But mature trees still in their prime rate as priceless assets. Call in a tree expert to check their health and to do any bolting or cabling needed.

Next check the shrubs. Age doesn't matter in shrubs. Healthy roots sprout out new

shoots if but stirred into action by a rich diet and a vigorous whacking back of the tops. Don't prune, though, until you have reviewed all your collection. Overgrown, leggy shrubs might well become important junior-size trees if pruned back to a few big shoots. Other shrubs might best be cut back into espalier forms.

Ignore existing perennial flowers at this stage of your planning. They move easily, shouldn't limit your thinking.

Fences, paths, and driveways also should be considered expendable. They probably need expensive repairs anyhow.

Now the way is cleared to think about what you want the new garden to do for you. Let this decide what to add to what you have saved. The next nineteen pages show what successful remodelers have done.

Now there is a way to descend from the automobile, proceed under cover to the new front door at what had been the back of the house.

Garden by Kathryn I. Stedman

Remodeling the old garden

Old concrete paving, even though broken into irregular pieces, can be relaid random-style for an informal terrace. Fine white marble goddess of gardens, Hsi Wang Mu, was saved from owner's old garden.

Street walls remains from the old garden, as is concrete-and-iron plaque by Florence Swift, but owner Church designed new light fixture of arching bronze tubing. Messy overgrowth of old ivy vine has been tamed into impressive display.

Garden by Thomas D. Church

This was a mess of tree branches, paths, and flower beds, seldom used because it failed to invite owners to live outdoors, lacked style to be attractive to guests.

Terrace now 70 feet wide dominates grounds in remodeled garden. Divider strips in paving lead your eyes out to swimming pool saved from old garden (see below).

New paving ties everything together, makes inviting paths to lead people through the garden. Pattern for exposed-aggregate concrete paving was planned so all lines join pleasantly, typical of details to remember.

Many old gardens are too big to maintain today when competent garden help is rare. Owner here decided to garden only as much of the lot as he thought he would be able to use and to care for himself. Don't be tempted to tackle too much just because so much exists in the way of fine old trees and shrubs. Consider what you want to do.

Look around for ways to give yourself a choice of small "rooms," a consideration often overlooked in another day when it was fashionable to try for an estate look of sweeping bigness, long vistas, great openness. Handsome doors here were salvaged from a saloon about to be torn down.

Let the location of existing trees determine where and what shape the outdoor dining room will take. You can pave right up to a tree without harm to it if you leave the grade undisturbed and the paving joints open.

Floor a heavily used area, here bricks on bed of sand, instead of struggling with grass. Confine lawn to non-traffic areas.

Privacy without annoying the neighbors is not always easy, but without privacy garden has little usefulness. Open-grid brick wall provides practical way to remain gracious here.

Garden by Joseph O. Lambert, Jr.

All that remains of a city lot—a back yard 30 by 50 feet, now lush all summer and for minimum upkeep, really useful to its owners, glamorous enough for party-giving.

Garden by Thomas D. Church

Garden by Thomas D. Church

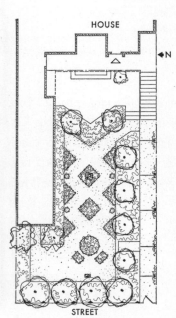

This is the Thomas Church residence. The garden was built in 1934, formal with boxwood hedges and white peacocks.

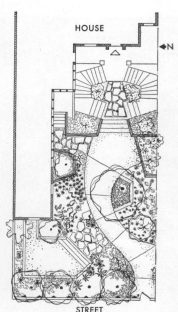

The 1954 garden shows a completely new concept, freer, more open, leading itself to a variety of moods but still formal in intent.

Restyled in 1950, with the formality eroded away by the exuberance of growth, and the glare of white fence toned down by diamond patterns of ivy, garden looked fresh.

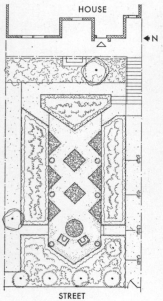

Terraces seldom are built large enough. This one seemed big to owner when built but less than ten years later was made several times larger. Safe rule: make terrace at least 2 to 3 times size of biggest room indoors, more if you can find space.

Garden by Douglas Baylis

Clearing away scattered trees and shrubs was first step in garden remodeling here. This freed open space for play equipment, also a swimming pool in the background.

The best trees were saved. Their positions determined the shape of such important additions as the zigzag bench. Elsewhere desirable shrubs were regrouped and reused.

Now yard affords off-street parking and a greatly simplified, easier-to-maintain planting at the front entrance. Big masses of evergreen here are spreading junipers.

Garden by Thomas D. Church

Remodeling the old garden

Pool is at new front entrance. Area was originally the back yard. Planting is lush but does not introduce burdensome upkeep because actual area is kept small.

Chinese mood of this remarkable old house sets the tone for the new garden just added. Indoors and out, colors are muted but cheerful Simplicity gives feeling of great repose. Spirit of the old was brought up to date without destroying its quality.

Garden by Ralph Smith

Ramp solved problem of differing grade levels that once checked free movement of people and equipment. Handsome pattern in paving for ramp makes the solution seem a feature of the new garden.

Deck lifts the new garden up to floor level, a solution shown in use in many situations in chapter 16, pages 330–349.

Big trees often contribute a kind of beauty available from no other source, yet so often nondescript, overgrown old shrubs bury this potential beauty. Garden remodelers should treasure every tree, look with questioning upon shrubs that hide the tree trunks. Sometime, big shrubs contribute more importantly when pruned into tree form, exposing their own quite sizable trunks. At other times clearing out a whole area to get free lawn (above) or place for a paved terrace (left) offers more beauty.

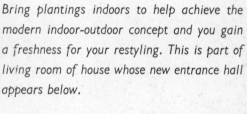

Bring plantings indoors to help achieve the modern indoor-outdoor concept and you gain a freshness for your restyling. This is part of living room of house whose new entrance hall appears below.

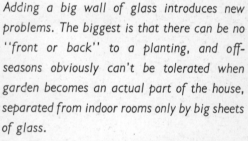

Adding a big wall of glass introduces new problems. The biggest is that there can be no "front or back" to a planting, and off-seasons obviously can't be tolerated when garden becomes an actual part of the house, separated from indoor rooms only by big sheets of glass.

The old foundation planting naturally has to go. A few choice plants replace it, chosen because their intrinsic beauty is exciting, positioned with infinite care to bring out all the beauty, be it from rugged outline or delicate tracery pattern. When your garden becomes a real part of your daily living, you must have something worth looking at year round.

Garden by Wendell R. Gilbert

Whatever is available, try to imagine it in new ways. A big perennial border, too costly to maintain today in the meticulous, planned sequence of color and season, might make a handsome, even ravishing if unorthodox, mass of mixed bloom when left to determine its own composition by natural reseeding rather than planned and enforced design and choice of plants, colors, and sizes.

Trees might better be left in broad sweeps of mowed grass, or left to grow in woodland glades without grass. Circumstances alter the choice of which is easier to maintain. Both can be beautiful.

Most mistakes in garden remodeling occur in deciding how much to keep. Most people find themselves unable to dig up or chop down ''perfectly good plants.'' The cost of this mistake is enormous. Better to err on the side of too extensive removal. You can always replace if in time you find the garden too bare, but your troubles just grow worse if you leave too many plants. Rules are risky, but if you remove ruthlessly to a bare minimum—then remove half of this—you'll come out about right. Better still, consult a landscape architect. He'll have no qualms about removing what should come out.

This house enjoys the most distinctive setting on the street, simplicity itself but so stylish that the age of the house seems unimportant. Involved are two ideas worth wide usage. First, the trees were pruned up to allow sunlight and shadows to fall upon the lawn. Second, the exposed foundation of the house was painted black to make it less conspicuous, eliminating any need for a high foundation planting. Now remaining evergreens call attention to the front door, make you less aware of the many jogs and setbacks in the house.

Garden by George Siebenthaler

Appendix I

MINIMUM 4' WIDE

DRESSED STONES
LAID UP IN MORTAR

Step-building involves principles of both engineering and pyschology, for steps work for us physically and emotionally. Steps may move us up or down in a businesslike way, or let us sweep down like royalty, seemingly float like a Peter Pan, or go so unnoticed that we are unaware of them. Ideal dimensions depend upon the site and the proposed reason for the steps. Dimensions here indicate ranges commonly found. Relationship between tread width and riser height should be altered to fit needs of the people who will use the steps most. Try various combinations until you find the one best for your needs (carry a tape measure and check the combination when you find it in steps or stairs you regularly use around town).

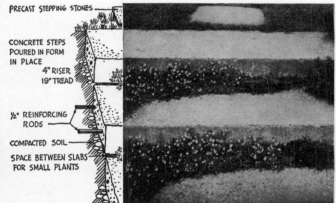

PRECAST STEPPING STONES

CONCRETE STEPS
POURED IN FORM
IN PLACE
4" RISER
19" TREAD

½" REINFORCING
RODS

COMPACTED SOIL

SPACE BETWEEN SLABS
FOR SMALL PLANTS

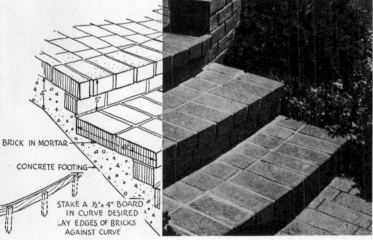

BRICK IN MORTAR

CONCRETE FOOTING

STAKE A ½" x 4" BOARD
IN CURVE DESIRED
LAY EDGES OF BRICKS
AGAINST CURVE

5"

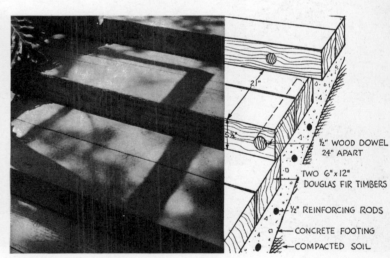

21"

½" WOOD DOWEL
24" APART

TWO 6"x 12"
DOUGLAS FIR TIMBERS

½" REINFORCING RODS

CONCRETE FOOTING

COMPACTED SOIL

3" RIVER-WASHED STONE
MORTAR JOINTS
(DEEP RAKED)

5" RISER
15" TREAD

USE ONE LAYER STONE
UNDER STEP

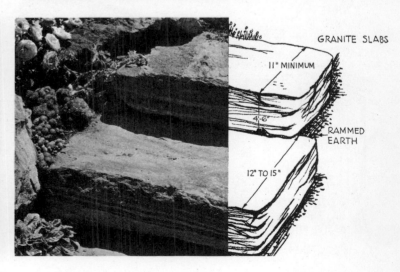

GRANITE SLABS

11" MINIMUM

4-6"

RAMMED
EARTH

12" TO 15"

Garden steps by Thomas D. Church

How to create pattern in your paving

STONE SLAB

USED BRICK INSERT (NO MORTAR)

3" SAND BED

USED BRICK PAVING ON SAND

Laying of paving involves far less engineering ability than most people think. Put down a base of concrete (bought ready-mixed as delivered—you merely level out) or a base of sand, then go to work with your finish paving. Work within grids to make keeping lines straight an easier chore. Choose a simple pattern for the first project, reserving cut flagstones, etc., for later times.

BRICK SET IN BASKET PATTERN; SAND SWEPT IN JOINTS

SAND BED

PRE-CAST CONCRETE, TERRAZZO, OR WOOD STRIPS TO GIVE PATTERN CONTRAST

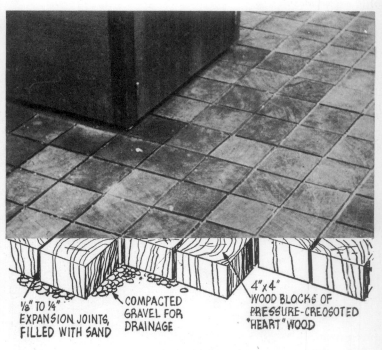

⅛" TO ¼" EXPANSION JOINTS, FILLED WITH SAND

COMPACTED GRAVEL FOR DRAINAGE

4"X 4" WOOD BLOCKS OF PRESSURE-CREOSOTED "HEART" WOOD

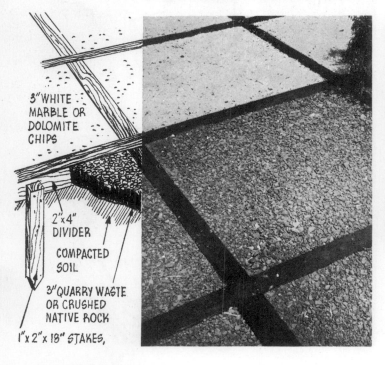

3" WHITE MARBLE OR DOLOMITE CHIPS

2"x 4" DIVIDER

COMPACTED SOIL

3" QUARRY WASTE OR CRUSHED NATIVE ROCK

1"x 2"x 18" STAKES,

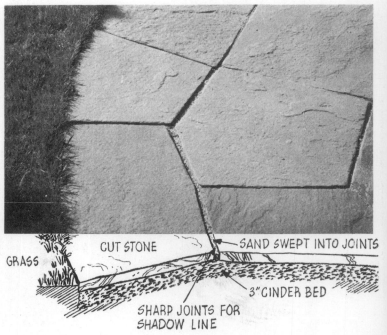

CUT STONE

SAND SWEPT INTO JOINTS

GRASS

SHARP JOINTS FOR SHADOW LINE

3" CINDER BED

Level the base sand a final time just before setting the brick. Check level of finished paving regularly: should slope slightly to drain.

Tamp brick to settle firmly on sand. Spacing bricks as here is tricky for beginner: better to butt bricks tightly the first time.

Use a chisel to cut bricks for fitting.

"Cut" all four sides, then give one sharp blow.

Fill joints with sand, slightly moistened.

Sweep away excess sand, exposing joints.

Wash remaining sand into the joints.

Firm sand in joints. Stay off paving 3 to 4 days.

It has been the author's pleasure to spend time in American gardens with many of the country's great garden photographers in preparing more than 4000 pictures, for *House Beautiful* magazine, 850 of which are represented in this book.

The Photographers

About

Maynard Parker: Few photographers have visited as many American gardens as this distinguished architectural photographer, himself a skilled amateur gardener. Native of Vermont, resident of Los Angeles since 1920, he visited all forty-eight states while preparing this collection, begun in 1946. He and the author also visited Central Mexico, as well as Eastern and Western Canada for garden photographs included here.

About

Gottscho-Schleisner: Native New Yorkers, they have photographed many of America's greatest estate gardens, now devote most of their time to gardens of the type which we call The New American Garden, especially in its more naturalistic forms. They and the author spent many delightful days making the seventy-three photographs included here.

The garden designers

Baker, Florence—111

Baylis, Douglas—8, 25, 101, 105, 107, 110, 116, 191(2), 269, 280, 281, 290, 291(2), 294, 342, 344(3), 345(2), 362(2), 367(2)

Beeson, Kenneth—234

Berger, Marie & Arthur—10, 19, 77(2), 127(6), 131(2), 132, 138, 144, 154(2), 158, 159, 160, 164(2), 165(2), 172(2), 173(2), 175, 184, 210, 211, 296(4), 297(3), 298(2), 299, 300(2), 301(3), 322, 323(2)

Berkeley Women's City Club—272

Bettencourt, Manuel—139

Bliss, Houston B.—322, 323(2)

Bowen, Natalie G.—196

California Landscape Society—54

Carmack, John—252, 253(2)

Cascio, Peter—112

Cattell, Mary D.—145

Champlin, Hannah—14, 78, 286

Church, Thomas D.—13(2), 15, 18(5), 20(2), 21(3), 22(3), 23, 24, 26(2), 27(3), 28, 29, 30(3), 31(3), 32(2), 33(2), 34(2), 35(3), 38, 39, 44, 46(3), 47(4), 48(2), 49, 51, 52, 55, 59, 60(1), 61, 77, 79(3), 80(3), 81(3), 83, 92, 93, 94(2), 95(5), 97(3), 116, 117, 118, 119, 120(2), 121, 125, 136, 137, 139, 149, 154(2), 155(2), 166, 170(4), 171(2), 175, 180, 181(3), 182(2), 183, 186(2), 187(2), 188, 190(2), 192(2), 193(4), 195(2), 200(3), 201(3), 207, 214, 216, 218, 219, 220(8), 221, 222(4), 223(4), 224(2), 225, 226(3), 227(3), 228, 229, 234, 242, 243(3), 246, 260(2), 266, 268(2), 269(3), 281(2), 282, 284, 288(3), 289(2), 293(6), 295, 308(3), 309, 312(2), 314(2), 315(3), 316, 317, 324(2), 325(2), 326, 328, 332, 338(5), 339, 350(2), 351(2), 354(2), 355(3), 358(2), 360, 361(3), 363(3), 371(6)

Cowan, James—275

Dalsimer, Allen—185, 204, 214, 311(2), 330, 334(3)

Darling, Janet—169, 303

Deering, Robert—136, 270

DeForest, Lockwood—208(4)

Dodge, Homer K.—15, 45(3)

Dudley, Leavitt—248

Eckbo, Royston & Williams—56(2), 57(2), 109(2), 202, 218, 235, 236, 237, 240(2), 241, 244, 249

Esherick, Ruby—146(2), 147

Fanning, James, & Johnson, Philip—209

Forr Landscape Nursery—12, 17, 44, 245

Fehr & Granger—273

Ferracone, E. A.—78, 219, 242

Fitch, James M.—267, 320(2)

Frankl, Paul—228, 229

Funk, John—275

Furlong, Ethelbert E.—55, 70, 73, 75, 87, 89, 91, 98(2), 99

Gerke, Florence & Walter—15, 66(3), 67(2), 68(2), 106, 232

Gilbert, Wendell R.—23, 117

Goodman, Charles—11

Grant, John—53, 112, 329

Greeley, Rose—302

Hajjar, A. W.—194

Halprin, Larry—25, 29, 62(2), 108, 115, 152, 249, 292(3), 293, 305

Hannastrom, Don—244

Harris, Harwell H.—287

Hill, John D.—198(3)

Holmdahl, Otto—45

Hoy, George—43

Huebsch, W. A.—245

Huntsman-Trout, Edward—14, 50, 58, 113, 136, 231, 284

Hutchinson, Paul—212(2)

Imlay & Scott—69(2), 177, 279(2), 290, 291

Johnston, Marian—102

Kelly, Thomas S.—154(2), 155(2)

King, John L.—106, 321(2)

Kruegal, George—278

Kuhlman, Richard A.—250, 251(2)

Lambert, Joseph O., Jr.—88, 356(2), 357(3)

Linder, Bertram—213

Lynch, Bryan, J.—285

May, Ruth—195(2)

McDonnell, Jack—93

Merrill, Vincent—43, 261, 264 265(3)

Mick, Floyd—52

Mosher, Robert—107, 219, 310

Oakland Business Men's Garden Club—214

Osmundson & Staley—82, 109, 110, 136, 139, 143(3), 189(4), 218, 242, 252, 280, 305, 337

Parker, Alfred B.—100(2)

Patterson, Ruth—158, 159, 160, 164(2), 165(2)

Peart, Paul J.—107

Pendleton, Isabella—72, 76

Prentice, Clarence—36(2), 37, 64(2), 65(2), 103, 307

Rarig, Ann—55

Rose, James—258, 259

Rosedale (N.Y.) Landscape Nursery—254, 336(3), 337

Royston, Robert—45, 274

Rucker, Ned—25, 176, 191, 218, 256, 257

Scott, Geraldine—207

Sheets, Millard—201, 205(2), 340

Shepherd, Harry W.—248

Shurcliff & Shurcliff—26

Siebenthaler, George—45, 305, 370

Smith, Ralph—261(2), 262(2), 364(2), 365(2)

Smith & Williams—199(3)

Stanton, Robert—134, 135, 156, 157

Stedman, Kathryn I.—108, 274, 280, 352, 353

Swift, Florence—184

Thiry, Paul—266

Tyler, Ted—209

Underhill, Stanley—316, 317

Wallace, R. & Co.—103

Walp, Don—38

Ward, Robertson—197(3)

Webel & Innocenti—14, 15(3), 40(3), 42(2), 117, 126, 128(4), 130(4), 132, 133(2), 255, 332, 333(2), 359

Wertheim, Ernest—304

Williams, Paul—60

Wimmer, Harriet—207, 209

Windemere, Thomas—273

Wright, Frank L.—104, 167, 169, 272, 347,

Wyatt, Edwin T.—84, 86(2), 106, 335(2), 341

Yeon, John—73, 78, 306

Yoch & Council—137

Index

Page numbers refer to either text or illustrations.

8593